# Heritage Pubs
# of Great Britain

# Heritage Pubs
# of Great Britain

*A photographic record by*

MARK BOLTON

*with introduction and commentaries by*

JAMES BELSEY

CAMRA
BOOKS

*Dedication*

*This book is dedicated to all lovers of the British pub at its best and its most authentic.*

*In a rapidly changing world which has seen more and more threats to this cornerstone of the British social scene, examples of the real British pub somehow manage to survive, their traditions, decor and architecture nurtured by gifted licensees and discerning customers.*

*The campaign for real ale - and traditional cider - continues apace. The campaign to protect a heritage of hospitality and pub architecture is its natural ally.*

*Long live the real British pub.*

*James Belsey and Mark Bolton, 1998.*

Published by CAMRA Books, Campaign for Real Ale,
230 Hatfield Road, St Albans AL1 4LW
Tel: 01727 867201  Fax: 01727 867670
Managing Editor: Mark Webb

Design: Patrick Harrison
Illustrations: Richard Coy

ISBN 1-85249-146-9

First Edition, November 1998

Great effort has gone into researching the contents of this book, but no responsibility can be taken for errors.
Printed and bound by The Bath Press, Bath

# Contents

# The Pubs

# *Introduction*

HERITAGE PUBS *of Great Britain* is a celebration . . . but it is also, inevitably, something of a lament. It celebrates the looks and striking character of some of those surviving traditional pubs which give so much pleasure and satisfaction to discerning drinkers throughout the United Kingdom. There are still, thankfully, a number of survivors of this grand tradition. They come in all shapes and sizes, from spartan but friendly country pubs to gloriously elaborate city ale houses.

But there is a sadder sub-text – a hidden lament for those countless, much-loved pubs which have been altered, themed up, sometimes re-named, often disfigured to suit a corporate image or, sadly, closed altogether.

The Campaign for Real Ale has fought a long and successful battle to draw the public's attention to the threats which face real ale. The pubs and their interiors depicted in this book are taken from CAMRA's National Inventory of Pub Interiors which has been painstakingly collated by the CAMRA Pubs Group over many hours, indeed years of discussion, surveying and argument. The National Inventory, which is given in full at the rear of the book, flags up pubs with interiors of outstanding historical interest.

The place of the real British pub in our island history is equally ancient. Pubs at their best lie at the heart of the community, whether in remote hamlets or in the rush and bustle of our great cities. They provide a touchstone for local people and visitors alike. Where else could you find a friendly, relaxing place to meet both friends or strike up a conversation with complete strangers in interesting, often highly individualistic surroundings?

The architecture and decoration play an important part in that free-and-easy atmosphere, creating an ambience that encourages talk and conviviality. No template exists, although today's pub designers think

The Three Stags Heads
DERBYSHIRE

they know the secret. How could they? How can you pin down the nature of a real British pub when what you are seeking is that elusive balance between hospitality, local character and appearance in very different settings. It is a quality which takes years of care to develop.

The sheer variety of these pubs is one of the treasures of Britain. How can you compare the palatial extravagance of The Crown Liquor Saloon in Belfast or the glittering, mirrored interior of The Red Lion in St James, just off Piccadilly with the yeoman charms of simple country inns like The Dyffryn Arms, set in its quiet valley in West Wales or The Peyton Arms, the social hub of a tiny Oxfordshire hamlet. The first two were created as triumphant, superbly detailed architectural entities by dedicated teams of skilled craftsmen. The latter pair have gradually perfected their simple appeal and rustic appearance over the decades, the basic fabric of the buildings largely

unaltered and their decoration only undergoing small changes as succeeding generations of licensees add their own personal touches in an evolving process of trial and error.

But what is common to all the pubs in this book – and the rest of the real British pubs of architectural interest which have managed to survive reasonably intact – is a sense of integrity which is immediately apparent the moment you step through the door. The devotee will recognise this quality before he or she even reaches the bar on a first visit. A brief glance around the interior brings a warm glow of satisfaction. Ah . . . now this is what I call a pub!

Another common characteristic is a tangible feeling of continuity, in unspoilt features and furniture and, in many cases, a family tradition of ownership which stretches back for generations and which has done so much to help preserve and nurture the character of a pub with all its foibles.

The 26 pubs and inns featured in this book, so beautifully illustrated by my colleague Mark Bolton's evocative photographs, are particularly special. Mark, a real pub enthusiast, wears his heart on his sleeve by superbly capturing their individuality and atmosphere for us all to enjoy.

There is, of course, a negative side to this story of the real British pub. It is that sickening sense of dismay and betrayal when a favourite is revisited, only to discover that its interior and decor have been altered irreparably and its unique attractiveness destroyed. It requires surprisingly little effort to wreck the spirit of the pub.

I have suffered two such losses in the past few years. One was a decent little watering hole in Knightsbridge, just around the corner from Harrods in central London. I'd used it on and off since the early 1960s. It was a friendly, welcoming, unpretentious, typical London pub. No longer. It has now been turned into a so-called "Irish" theme pub. Genuine character has been stripped away by corporate revisionism and "character" – in inverted commas – introduced. Real Irish pubs are a revelation. There is a small problem, however: they are all to be found in Ireland, not in central London. The cuckoo had entered the nest and I walked away.

Even worse – because it had been my local for more than 30 years – was the fate of the small but famous cider pub, The Coronation Tap in the beautiful Georgian/Regency suburb of Clifton in Bristol. This classic little pub, set incongruously among the terraces and crescents in Clifton, was a gem. Its two intimate rooms were softly lit by daylight during the day and a warm glow of artificial light by night. It had remained little change for decades and its admirers, not just from Bristol but from across the country and even overseas, loved its rough simplicity. They helped ensure a ceaseless, welcoming background of talk and laughter as they sipped real cider and ale. Barristers rubbed shoulders with builders, university professors swapped anecdotes with garage mechanics, the occasional famous actor from the adjoining BBC radio studios would wander in and we were all the better for each others' company and our surroundings. Gone, all gone. In a single clumsy stroke walls were broken down to double the drinking area and the intimacy we had all found so appealing was consigned to history. Its regulars, famous, infamous and anonymous, fled like swallows seeking warmth elsewhere. Today the windows shed no light into extension, leaving The Tap gloomy and depressing by daytime and, at night, the haunt of deafening hordes of students drinking powerful, fizzy bottled cider on empty heads.

Every CAMRA supporter will have similar horror stories to tell: noisy juke boxes replacing pub pianos, plastic settees rammed into corners once occupied by cosy, well-worn wooden settles, charming little snug bars ripped out to maximise the drinking area, ancient features cladded over with faceless chipboard. The list is endless.

The Sixties may have been a golden era for creativity in Britain. Not, I fear, for real British pubs. That was when the decline began in earnest.

There is no single villain of the piece. Brutalist breweries, eager to make the very most of their assets and their powerful monopolies, have a lot to answer for. The marketing-led drive from licensee to manager in a successful attempt to centralise control, delivered a body blow to many, many pubs. The close relationship between landlord and customer was eroded. A successful licensee knows and understands the likes and dislikes of his or her customers and reacts to them with sensitivity. The temporary manager and brewery head office cannot possibly understand this delicate balance on which real pubs have always thrived.

This move to managed houses went hand in hand with a heavily financed promotional drive to make us accept the bland fizz of keg beer and cider. It made a lot of sense back in the head offices of the big brewers. Why waste time on brewing real ale and training licensees in the art of caring for and correctly serving these ales and ciders if you could persuade punters to accept anodyne alternatives which required no cellar skills at all?

It was a local step from the so-called "keg revolution" to the bland, corporate interior. Frankly, they deserved each other.

Slack, lazy licensees and managers have much to answer for. They contributed to the decline not only with the sheer uncaring drabness of the decor but also with their disregard for the basic rules of hospitality. A defining study of this phenomenon was captured by the film-maker Dick Lester – no coincidence that he is American and was therefore able to take a more dispassionate view of the British pub than we were. It came in A Hard Day's Night, his 1964 movie with the

Beatles. There is a perfectly observed scene in which an errant Ringo Starr wanders into a London pub for a pint, a sandwich and a game of darts. Surly locals glare at him, the sandwiches are stale and mine hostess is a Gorgon. Ringo is utterly frozen out and finally banned from the premises. Anyone who remembers 1960s pubs at their grimmest – and heavens knows there were enough of them – will recognise the scene at once.

The Sixties also saw the start of the demise of the lounge bar, the slightly smarter room where drinks cost a penny or two more but where couples could drink in comfort while the talk and behaviour in the adjoining public bar were more down-to-earth. Down came the walls in pubs across the country.

The curious licensing laws of the time – a puritanical left-over from World War I when bossy politicians decreed that the free-and-easy days of all-day opening posed a threat to the war effort – and radical changes in our everyday lives brought other pressures. As more and more Britons took foreign holidays, we began to discover that there was more to life than stale ham sandwiches, suspicious-looking pork pies and a possibly dodgy welcome over a pint of belch-making fizzy beers.

A new breed of caterer saw the clear opportunities offered by the decline of the British pub in the 1960s and eagerly – and successfully – moved in with wine bars, bistros and other competition. British pubs lost their monopoly of drinks and simple food at reasonable prices.

Those stalwarts running thriving real pubs – bless them – soldiered on, keeping their traditions alive and earning the thanks of real ale and cider enthusiasts. CAMRA has fought hard to support them, drawing attention to outstanding pubs with its Good Beer Guides and other publications. What CAMRA began, others followed and today we have a proliferation of similar guides, books and regular pub feature articles in national and regional newspapers and magazines.

Finding a decent pub used to be a hit-and-miss affair. It isn't any longer.

But despite this growing awareness of our pub heritage, the list of casualties grows. Yesterday's fad – to the embarrassment of our cousins across the Irish Sea – was the Irish theme pub, a travesty of the real thing. The American bar is now with us. Someone will no doubt come up with another theme before long, another marketing ploy which will find its victims in decent pubs.

I'm not a purist. A juke box with interesting records in the setting of a pub with a music tradition of folk, blues or jazz is not to be sniffed at. I prefer old-fashioned pub games like shove ha'penny, bar billiards and darts to flashy gaming machines but accept that, for some licensees, they are a commercial necessity.

But, like every real pub lover, I'm on the look-out for the genuine, the interesting, the unusual and a strong sense of identity and character. You don't, like some contempory pub interior designers, buy that sort of integrity by leafing through architectural reclamation company catalogues offering church pews and old shop fittings and installing period artifacts wholesale in a pub. You can see through the device easily and it is as phony as a mock-Georgian modern house.

The 26 pubs in this book all share this integrity and it is what makes them such an important part of British heritage. Heritage is a much over-used and abused word, I know, but here it is the truth.

During my chats with the licensees, particularly at country pubs, one point was made time and again. The landlords were anxious to stress that their premises are not museum pieces to be pickled in aspic but thriving, successful businesses which trade on their traditions and individual appeal. Furniture and fittings do sometimes need replacing when wear and tear has rendered them obsolete and, quite rightly, they demand the freedom to add their own touches.

The Black Horse
CLAPTON - in - GORDANO

Landlords also enjoy adding to the character of their pubs. The huge collection of key rings assembled at The Seven Stars in Falmouth, Cornwall is an amusing example of how a family, by chance, created a new tradition of their own. The collection of old firearms at The Black Horse in Clapton-in-Gordano in Somerset is an even more recent addition and it fits in very well. Going back further in time, the amazing Victorian egg collection at The Ship Hotel in Overton, Lancashire is one of The Ship's treasures.

The chance nature of country pub decoration is perfectly illustrated by the stag's skull which perches on a couple of coat hangers at The Square and Compass at Worth Matravers in Dorset. It was set up for a Halloween party, looked good and has somehow

never been taken down. In the same pub you'll find patriotic graffiti celebrating VE Day carved into a table.

The great city pubs have an altogether different tradition and here stricter rules must – and do – apply. The breathtaking interior of The Philharmonic in central Liverpool was created by a small army of Liverpool's most gifted decorative artists, men who had adorned the great luxury ocean liners of the day. Glasswork, carving, mosaics and woodwork come together in a riot of Victorian splendour. The intricate snug bars of The Prince Alfred in London's Maida Vale, complete with their curious little waist high interconnecting doors, are all of a piece. The Black Horse Hotel in Birmingham was built in the 1920s as a flagship for the brewers Davenports and no expense was spared in its rooms to make it one of Birmingham's finest. These buildings are now protected and listed as places of historical and architectural interest.

It was a Grade II listing that not only saved but restored The Kings Head in Bristol when it was threatened with demolition. To their credit, brewers Courage sent in builders who chipped away at scores of coats of paint to discover original fittings and surfaces that had lain hidden for decades and which are now there to be enjoyed in all their finery.

The listing of these grandiose buildings now ensures their future. It is less grand country cousins we need to cherish and to support. That point came home with great force during the preparation of this book. Mark Bolton's photographs of the modest, unassuming interior of The Berkeley Hunt on the banks of the Gloucester and Sharpness Canal are now a historical record. The pub is no more. Once a farmhouse, its owners decided to cash in on the building of the canal by taking out a licence in 1827 so that they could serve the army of navvies who had arrived in this corner of Gloucestershire and, later, the crews of passing boats

The Prince Alfred
Formosa Street, London

during the canal's heyday. Just months before the publication of this book the owners decided to call it a day. Pints are now longer poured in the corridor and the building has reverted to its original use as a farmhouse. Trade had dwindled to such an extent that it was no longer commercially viable to keep The Berkeley Hunt going as a pub.

In other rural communities, the villages themselves have undergone changes which have helped them survive and prosper. The Star in Netherton, Northumberland has a new influx of customers because Netherton has become a growing commuter area, the newcomers enjoying the old-fashioned delights of their little village pub.

Pubs have fought back in other ways. The atmosphere in many pubs is now, thankfully, far more woman-friendly. Wine lists have improved and so has the catering. Quiz nights, music evenings and other entertainments have been the salvation of many a decent pub and good luck to the enterprising licensees who have introduced them.

We should all be as optimistic as we can and there are good reasons for hope. Although threats continue to overshadow the future of many surviving real British pubs, the irony is that this is a period of great opportunity. The existence of pubs of the quality to be found in these pages is regularly highlighted by guides and articles. The anachronism of our World War I licensing has been swept away. Tourism and the search for Heritage Britain are one of our most successful modern industries and the British pub is just as important and integral a part of that as stately homes, Stonehenge and Shakespeare's Stratford-upon-Avon.

The future holds great promise for those who worked so hard to keep alive the tradition and spirit of the British pub at its best. They deserve all the support and encouragement we can give them – and, above all, they deserve our thanks.

# The Pubs

# The Peyton Arms

## STOKE LYNE · OXFORDSHIRE

THE BUSY M40 is barely a mile away. It impinges not at all on the tiny hamlet of Stoke Lyne and its utterly traditional little village pub named after a local land-owning family. Beer is served straight from the barrel in a small low servery behind the main bar. The walls are adorned with fine old photographs from Stoke Lyne's past with village scenes and pictures of the nearby railway.

Time-honoured pub games and puzzles are carefully preserved and enthusiastically played by locals and discerning pub-goers who make the pilgrimage along country lanes to enjoy a pint at The Peyton. Demonstrations of how to solve one puzzle, which involves perching 12 loose nails on a single fixed nail, are charged at 25p a time and this has proved a novel way of raising hundreds of pounds for charity. The Peyton dates back to the early 19th century but was probably built on the site of an

earlier inn. Today its two bars are furnished simply and authentically. The oak beam in the main bar is festooned with dried hops which are replaced annually. The little back bar, which is only open during the busy weekend, is a low-ceilinged sanctuary of rural peace and calm.

*Above: A small 1880s match striker celebrating the centenary of the Fletton brickworks. It is still in daily use.*
*Opposite: The main bar with traditional country pub furniture and a nostalgic collection of photographs depicting the life of the village and nearby countryside over the years. The dried hops on the main beam are replaced every year.*

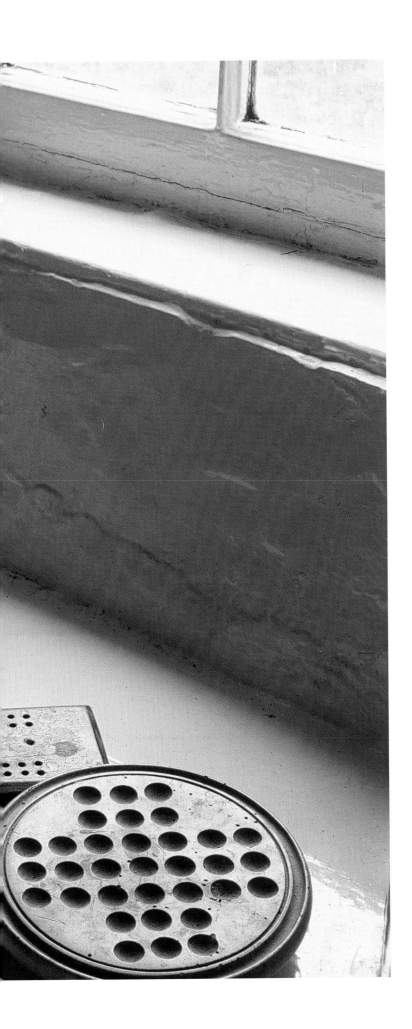

*Above: the real Dad's Army. The Stoke Lyne Home Guard proudly guarding the village church from any invaders.*

*Above: The weather-worn pub sign.*
*Left: The window sill of the main bar complete with a range of pub games and little puzzles. Dominos and other games are keenly played and one of the puzzles, involving perching 12 loose nails on a single fixed nail, is demonstrated to visitors for a charge of 25p a time, raising hundreds of pounds for charity over the years.*

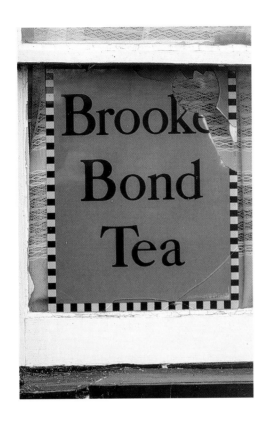

*Opposite: The little back bar which is only used at weekends. The low-ceilinged interior with its simple settles and other furniture, is a haven of rural peace for lovers of country pubs at their most traditional.*

*Above: An old advertising sign for Brooke Bond Tea.*

*Above right: A solitaire board, one of the pub's collection of games.*

*Below right: The 1806 builder's sign outside the pub, recording the date of the pub's construction. The Peyton Arms was probably built on the site of an earlier village inn.*

# The Antelope

BELGRAVIA • LONDON

HIDDEN AMONG the haughty white terraces and embassies of Belgravia, the spartan charm of The Antelope comes as a complete surprise. One of the oldest pubs in this part of London, The Antelope is a gathering place for City types and other locals who find relaxation in an atmosphere that seems miles away from the great squares and terraces outside. Half-panelled walls, a tongue-and-groove bar, a simple tiled fireplace and a rough pine bookcase for the solo drinker to choose a soothing volume to contemplate in an airy, well-lit pub provide a perfect distraction for those who cherish the authentic and the real in a dizzy world of high finance.

*Opposite: The back bar of The Antelope . . . comfortable armchairs, a tiled fireplace and a pine bookcase complete with books for browsers.*
*Above right: One of the traditional wooden country settles in the small side bar.*
*Below right: The front bar with its airy windows looking out to the lofty white buildings of Eaton Terrace.*

24

# The Berkeley Hunt

PURTON · GLOUCESTERSHIRE

EVEN AS THIS BOOK was in preparation, time was being called for the last time and the final pints served in The Berkeley Hunt's 170-year-old history as a canal-side village inn. Mark Bolton's photographs of the interiors are now a valuable record of a vanished chapter of Gloucestershire's social history and the building has now reverted to its original use as a farmhouse.

The inn opened in 1827 during the cutting of the adjoining Gloucester and Sharpness canal with the navvies calling in to quaff cider and beer and sate their appetites with bread and cheese. The late, redoubtable Kathleen Musselwhite took over the pub in this keen hunting area – hence the name – in the early 1950s and went on to become one of the country's oldest licensees, dispensing drinks from a counter in the little passageway between the public bar and the Smoke Room. The spartan interiors with their painted tongue-and-groove half-cladding, country furniture and traditional pub games like shove ha'penny delighted lovers of simple, unadorned country pub architecture and no less than 6 TV dramas featured The Berkeley Hunt, including the well-remembered police series Softly Softly. Sadly, a changing world saw a steady decline in trade until, reluctantly, Mrs Musselwhite's descendants decided to call it a day.

The pub fittings have gone, the days and nights of good ale and conversation between locals and passers-by are over. Yet another memorable part of our pub heritage has vanished.

*Opposite: The interior of the main public bar with simple tongue-and-groove wall cladding, clothes peg rail aloft, sturdy country chairs and table, a scoreboard on the wall and a shove ha'penny board on the table.*
*Above: The exterior of The Berkeley Hunt.*

*Above: A detail of the wallpaper featuring horses . . . the family breed prize-winning show ponies at what has now become Berkeley Hunt Farm.*

*Above: A photograph of a famous point-to-pointer West Point, taken shortly after World War II.*

*A detail of a curtain hanging in the main public bar, with beer glass. The interiors have been altered and the building has reverted to a private farmhouse.*

*Opposite: A view from the Public Bar across the passageway to the Smoke Room. Drinkers were served from a counter in the passageway to the right, opposite the front door to the inn.*

# The Harrow

STEEP • HAMPSHIRE

THE HARROW'S rural name reflects its position in the Hampshire countryside. The solitary building stands beside an ancient drovers' road along which cattlemen took their animals to country markets for many hundreds of years, perhaps even before Domesday. Parts of the building are Victorian to early 18th century, others are even older. There are two very small, intimate drinking areas, the original bar and another added in Victorian times. The public bar, the oldest part of the building, has a timelessness which reflects The Harrow's continuity and great age. Its beamed ceilings, large inglenook fireplace and simple servery decorated with garlands of home-grown hops greet drinkers today as they have for centuries. The smaller bar is known as The Smoking Room.

The pub has been run by the same family since 1926, since when little has changed. The furniture and fittings have been little altered, with additions only made when some piece needs replacing. A special feature are the stools in the public bar, fashioned out of solid trunks of oak and worn smooth by generations of bottoms over countless pints of beer. Unfussy, rough-hewn and basic, The Harrow is a model of traditional rustic hospitality which has been jealously guarded and cherished.

*Opposite: The rough surface of the old door to the little public bar, complete with its original door latch and hook and eye lock.*

*Opposite: The main, oak-beamed Public Bar with its large brick-built fireplace and massive beamed mantel. Open coal and wood fires are burnt throughout the colder weather to give the bar a much appreciated warmth. Notice the seats made from solid oak trunks, their surfaces smoothed by many years of use. The swags of dried hops festooning the servery are home-grown and replaced annually.*
*Below: A corner of a fire surround, installed in 1930. The pub has been in the same family since the 1920s and only small changes have been made over the years.*

*Above: Light pours through the square paned window of the main bar, lightening the interior and the dark beamed ceiling. Outside is an ancient drover's road, thought to date back to the days before Domesday.*
*Below: A detail of the plain tiled floor in the small Public Bar.*

*Opposite: Looking from the servery towards the window of the main Public Bar with simple high backed settles, basic tongue-and-groove pine walls, age-darkened oak beams and plain tables and benches. A collection of family photographs, local scenes and other pictures adorn the walls.*

*Above left: Another view of the main bar, looking towards the door to the second bar called The Smoking Room.*

*Centre: The richly grooved surface of a very heavy stool made from a solid piece of oak. Many of the stools in the pub are old oak logs.*

*Below left: An amusing little window display with toy sheep, reflecting the pub's rural setting in the Hamsphire countryside.*

# The Red Lion

SNARGATE · KENT

THE JEMISON FAMILY deserve the blessings of all lovers of traditional pubs for saving The Red Lion. In 1960 this ancient inn, said to date back to 1540, was saved from demolition when its landlord of the previous 49 years, Alfred Jemison, bought the business. It is still in the family and now run by his daughter-in-law Doris.

The title deeds show that in the 18th century it was a Romney Marsh coaching inn and a complete inventory made in 1911 when Alfred Jemison arrived proves that many of the fittings and furniture you will find today – including the oil lamp which hangs in the bar as well as marble-topped bar and chairs polished to a conker-like shine by more than 150 years of wear – are still. One of the newer additions include the bar till which arrived

*Above: A detail of a World War II poster appealing to the public to Dig for Victory.*

*Opposite: The bar-room, looking through to the parlour. Beer is gravity dispensed from barrels behind the wood-panelled and marble topped bar which is mentioned in an inventory made in 1911 when the Jemison family took over the pub.*

just after decimalisation – but still recording pounds, shillings and pence.

The clock, a French bagatelle board, the beer engine and many other items of furniture in the bar, bar parlour and tap room are also listed. The cellar lies beside the tap room – the water table of Romney Marsh does not allow for underground cellars.

Despite its antiquity, The Red Lion is no museum piece. Local pub games like toad-in-the-hole, a form of penny-tossing, are still played enthusiastically. Furniture is only replaced when necessary with suitable, practical alternatives as they always have been here . . . the pews in the tap room and parlour came from nearby Brookland Church.

As Mrs Jemisons says, Marsh people like to keep Marsh things on the Marsh.

Opposite: Interior with yellow light. Wood or coal fires burn here each winter. The wood-panelled passageway leads to the cellar and tap room where darts and the local game toad-in-the-hole are played.

Above left: An ancient ale and beer poster.

Above right: A 1977 photo of Mrs Jemison with her 'talking' labrador hangs from a Victorian coat hook.

Below left: Door to the bar with metal Old Holborn advertisement.

Below right: The 'White Stool' which belongs to a customer who will sit nowhere else.

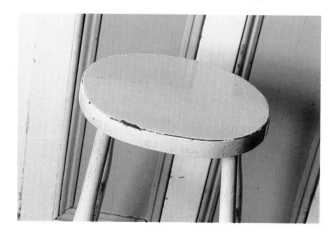

# The Star Inn

NETHERTON • NORTHUMBERLAND

THE CHARACTER of the village of Netherton has changed greatly recently with the influx of newcomers who commute daily to Newcastle, Sunderland, Jarrow and other nearby towns. The Star has not. Vera Wardley Wilson-Morton, who was born here and whose grandfather took over the licence in 1917, has altered little in her lifetime. The deeds of the building, which has three foot deep walls, date back to 1788 although the original two-room house was extended at the start of this century to make it, for a while, an hotel. Today there is a single public bar with a front door to both the bar and private living accommodation, the serving counter measuring a bare three feet. The Star is a country pub at its most ascetic. Polished brass bars protect the glass panel on the door to the bar, an assortment of old fashioned furniture, including settles and half-backed wooden armchairs, offer rest and relaxation, and a handsome advertisement for Ushers Pale Ale dominates the room.

*Opposite: The single bar at The Star Inn with half-backed armchairs and settles which continue along all the walls of the small room. Above: A detail of the Ushers mirror advertisement. Below left: Detail of the edge of one of the settles. Below right: A brass sign advertising The Star in its days as an hotel.*

*Above: A view of the bar, looking towards the entrance door. The settles line the walls of the single room with its three-foot-wide serving area.*

*Right: A detail of the door into the bar. The brass struts protect the glass panel of the upper door with, below left, a simple finger-plate.*

# The Black Horse

*Left: A collection of eight old fire-arms displayed aggressively over the large stone fireplace in the main bar. A simple bucket serves as the scuttle for the roaring open fire, well fed with rough-cut logs.*

*Horse brasses, darkened oak beams and panelling and plain country furniture set the style for this Grade II listed building.*

*Above: Walls are adorned with a variety of old brewery signs, landscapes, cigarette cards and other memorabilia.*

A SIMPLE, white-washed exterior, beer and cider directly from barrels in a traditional open serving area, flagstone floors, low ceilings, oak beams darkened by centuries and sturdy country furniture . . . step into the dappled interior of The Black Horse and you walk into a chapter of Somerset history.

Today the hillside village of Clapton overlooking the Gordano valley and the M5 motorway has been transformed into executive commuter-land for neighbouring Bristol. But once it was a mining village, with locals scratching a living from the coal they dug out of nearby shafts to be ferried across the Severn estuary to Wales. Few visitors realise the pub is named not after a handsome farming shirehorse but the wretched, coal-smeared pit ponies which worked alongside the equally grimy miners.

This 14th century, Grade II listed building probably began life as a farmhouse but has been a pub for several hundred years. It takes a keen eye to spot a poignant relic of social history in the Snug. The small window is barred . . . the room once had a dual role as both a bar and an overnight lock-up for miscreants. Succeeding generations of landlords have added their own personal touches, but always in keeping with the inn. A collection of musty firearms bristling above the large stone fireplace in the main bar look as if they had grown there and not been introduced relatively recently.

A handsome collection of cider mugs hang off dark oak beams, old brewery signs, framed groups of cigarette cards and other pictures adorn the walls. Light peeks through small windows into interiors that come alive to village gossip, the chatter of Bristolians on a night out in the country and the laughter of serious cider and beer drinkers who love the authenticity of real Somerset, not the picture postcard land of be-smocked, straw chewing yokels. The Black Horse reflects North Somerset as it really was.

*Above left: The Snug bar with its oak-beamed ceiling hung with a collection of traditional cider and beer mugs. Rustic tables and settles collected over the years give an air of true country pub authenticity . . . social historians will notice the small window with its metal bars. This room once served as the village lock-up in Clapton-in-Gordano's rougher days as a mining village.*

*Below left: The main bar with its dim interior, panelling, small tables and collection of pictures. The darkened walls and ceilings, flagstone floors and rustic simplicity combine to give The Black Horse a particularly rugged mood.*

*Opposite: The window of the main bar with old shutters and, left, an old poster for the long-gone George's Brewery of nearby Bristol.*

# The Crown Liquor Saloon

GREAT VICTORIA STREET · BELFAST

*Above: A glimpse into one of the eight little snug bars. Each has its own intimate atmosphere and design with richly decorated panelling inset with stained and engraved glasswork. Opposite: A detail showing just a small section of the superbly finished ceramic tiled floor. These highly-decorated triangular and diamond design tiled floors are to be found throughout the pub.*

FROM ITS STRIKING NAME, you might expect to be about to step into a Wild West saloon when you see the sign of this inn. Nothing could further from the reality of entering this palace of a city centre pub . . . and little wonder that the glories of The Crown Liquor Saloon have become a magnet for lovers of grandiose architecture and design from across the world. Not only is The Saloon owned and protected by the National Trust, it is also one of the rare pubs in the United Kingdom to have been rated as a Grade I listed buildings.

A somewhat humbler Crown Liquor was built and opened in 1849. Then, in 1880, it underwent a complete transformation when an army of skilled craftsmen set to work to create these High Victorian interiors with their ornate carved woodwork and glittering cut and stained glass. An intricate series of eight little interlocking snugs, guarded by carved heraldic beasts and beautifully furnished with richly decorated panelling and windows, rise from the elaborate mosaic floor with its diamond-shaped patterns.

*Opposite: Button-backed settles and the inviting, beautifully ornate mahogany surrounds of a pair of the snug bars, decorated with patterned details and insets of decorative glasswork. Each snug is guarded by a heraldic beast. The ceilings are of intricate plasterwork. The lamp in the corner, like all the lamps in the pub, are gas lit, creating a soft, golden light and deep shadows once the sun goes down.*

*Above right: A carved gryphon stands proudly and protectively above one of the snug bars, guardian of the privacy of the drinkers enjoying the comfort and opulence inside.*

*Right: A somewhat rueful bearded face, just one of hundreds of details on the stained glass exterior windows.*

*Opposite: The pub's name is reflected in a series of these stained glass crowns which adorn all of the exterior windows.*

*Right: The entrance to The Saloon, showing the intricate windows and a striking sign advertising high class whiskies and Sandeman's special wines.*

*Above: The narrow passage between two of the eight snug bars, a celebration of High Victorian pub architecture at its very best. All these interiors are strictly protected and preserved by the National Trust and The Saloon has a Grade I listing.*

*Right: One of the metal match strikers carefully screwed on to the walls to discourage thoughtless smokers from damaging the panels by carelessly striking a match on their elaborate surfaces.*

The detailing is exquisite and universal here, including the colourful crown motif resplendent on the main windows, old signs proclaiming high class whiskies and special wines and wonderful latticed doors which offer privacy and seclusion in the comfortable little snugs. There are even little match strikers screwed onto the panelling to prevent an unthinking smoker damaging the woodwork by striking a match on the mahogany surfaces.

And once the sun starts to set, a different magic takes over. The Saloon is gradually transformed from its sparkling day-time finery to a muted interior lit only by pale gas lamps, creating areas of shadow and soft light like some impressionistic painting.

# Ye Ole Tavern

## KINGTON · HEREFORDSHIRE

THE MODEST, DOUBLE-BAY fronted facade of Ye Ole Tavern gives no clue as to what lies inside . . . a true country pub, unfussy, welcoming and with a history that stretches back well over two centuries. It was called The Railway Tavern until the branch line to this little market town was closed in the 1950s and the name Ye Ole Tavern adopted. It is a fitting title. The inn almost certainly stood by itself surrounded by fields a century before the railway arrived in the 1870s and it is recorded as long ago as 1767. The facade is a later addition, disguising the simpler architecture within. The two panelled and half-panelled bars, the public and the lounge, each have

*Left: A corner of the panelled bar complete with traditional four-legged stools.*
*Right: The double-bayed exterior, a later addition to the traditional country inn. The public bar is to the left, the lounge to the right.*

their own bay window. The furnishings and decor is as rural as you could hope for, with furniture and curios lovingly collected over the years including Royal mugs, an ancient cigarette packet, old notices, 1960s ash trays and, blessedly, an upright piano rather than the ubiquitous juke box. A brass-framed sign over the fireplace celebrates the granting of the 100th licence to the Jones family in 1984. The last of the Jones licensees died five years later but the tradition they fostered lingers on, untouched by modernity. Locals gather to chat, relaxing in high-backed wooden settles and around a collection of wooden tables or on wooden stools at the bar. The harmony is

'The Smallest Bottle
of Scotch Whisky
in the World...?'

*Opposite: Some of Ye Ole Tavern's memorabilia including Royal commemorative mugs and a tiny whisky bottle box.*

*Above: a chair and door detail.*

*Above right: The unspoilt lounge bar complete with its ancient settle to the left and, to the right, the pub's dart board. The room also has an upright piano for sing-songs.*

*Right: More memorabilia . . . a worn packet of Woodbine Export cigarettes.*

*Below right: The patina of age on a handle.*

# The Red Lion

## ST JAMES · LONDON

THIS JEWEL-BOX OF A PUB sparkles with ornate mirrors, decorative glass, the glitter of brass and veneer of hand-carved mahogany, polished lovingly for more than a century. It has been the haunt of the rich and famous, the not-so-famous and even the poor since Victorian times. Oscar Wilde, a habitue in his heyday, must have given his seal of approval to the sheer sumptuousness of this exotic interior, now – quite rightly – Grade II listed. Today's glitterati visitors include Clint Eastwood, Mel Gibson, Andrew Lloyd-Webber – all recent clients. American guide book raves ensure a

regular flow of transatlantic visitors who are as bewitched as the natives by this beautiful survivor of a very different age. Time has wrought changes . . . the original lay-out with its series of very private little snugs separated by screens and curtains has given way to a more open plan with two main bars at the front and back but the mirrors with their various

*Opposite: A detail of what remains of the cut glass partition to what was once one of several intimate snug bars at The Red Lion. The snugs have been replaced by a more open plan.*
*Above: The exterior of The Red Lion. The ancient cellars run beneath Duke of York Street.*

floral patterns and the mahogany is original. Note the serpentine back bar carved from a single piece of wood. In Victorian times the snugs separated the classes: trades people in one area, the gentry in another. So private were some of the rooms that not long ago one little old lady confessed that in her youth she supplemented her meagre income as a flower seller by a little hanky-panky with toffs - at a modest cost. Today that intimacy has gone but the openness allows visitors to marvel at the overall impact created by the designers and craftsmen who transformed a much older building into high Victorian camp.

*Opposite: The front bar looking out towards Duke of York Street. The elaborate mahogany bar and its details, the decorative mirrors and the cut glass are all original, dating back 150 to 160 years. Oscar Wilde regularly drank here during walks through St James.*

*This page: Details of the interior including the pub clock and some of the cut glass windows, each window featuring a different type of flower.*

# The Kenilworth

EDINBURGH'S The Kenilworth is named after the 1821 novel by the celebrated Scottish writer Sir Walter Scott, who lived around the corner. Walter Scott was fascinated by history and period settings and set his tragic romance in English Elizabethan times. The Kenilworth has a perfect, though later, period setting too. A Grade A listed building, its florid Edwardian interior with tiled walls, lofty decorative mirrors and a host of flourishes and architectural details, is now one of Edinburgh's greatest attractions for lovers of ornate city taverns. The foliate carving on the bar and other wooden fittings is superbly finished, and airy windows brighten the interior with a luscious sparkle. Some of the carving on the bar is echoed by the matching design of the wrought iron legs of both the tables and stools. The property itself dates back to 1789 and had a chequered history, serving at various times as a private house and even an abbatoir. It did not become a pub until 1904 when the present interior was designed and installed. Right in the very heart of the city – Edinburgh's popular Princes Street is just a stone's throw away – The Kenilworth is a celebration of Edwardian splendour at its best.

*Opposite: A foliate detail from the elaborate carved wood bar which looks out into Rose Street, with below it, one of the original, ornate glass mirrors, and wooden seats at the bar . . . the wrought-iron legs use a design echoing details of the carved woodwork of the bar.*
*Above: The tall windows and seating area which overlook Rose Street.*

# The Star

## BATH · SOMERSET

SET AMONG the cosmopolitan Georgian and Regency splendours of central Bath's world-famous architecture, the small, compact Star has a simplicity and charm all of its own, making this a favourite refuge for locals as they escape the crush and crowds of life in one of the world's most popular and busy tourist attractions.

The Star's history as a pub is a venerable one. It was first licensed as a public house in the 1760s. There are no grapes grown or wine made on its adjoining hillside today, but instead what its devoted regulars will tell you are the city's finest pints of Bass, served in time-honoured fashion in four-pint jugs.

The building itself is far older than its rather grander neighbours, including such fine examples of Georgian architecture as The Paragon, on which work began half a dozen or so years after The Star opened its doors as an inn. The original entrance to the pub is now at the rear while today's front door opens out on to the main road below.

Many period interior details have remained unaltered for more than a century, including 19th century bar fittings which were made by Gaskells and Chambers of Dale End, Birmingham. The landlord still transports barrels from the cellar to the bar area using a lift which rises through a trapdoor set in the bar floor.

All this could have vanished in a moment in 1942 during the so-called Baedeker raids when houses directly opposite suffered a direct hit. The Star emerged virtually unscathed.

*Opposite: A view from the corner of "Glass Room" bar, looking across to the smallest bar, a long narrow room furnished only with a long bench. The bench is the seat of choice for many older regulars and is affectionately known by them as "Death Row". A communal tin of snuff can always be found in the little bar, resting on a ledge of the wall panelling.*

Opposite: *View across the pumps into the main bar, furnished with two large rectangular tables. The books are cricketing memoirs and humorous works collected over the years by the pub's cricket club.*

Above: *The brass plate on the door to the Glass Room.* Below left: *A window above the long bench known as "Death Row". This is the entrance on the Paragon and the frosted glass is decorated with a star motif.*
Below right: *An old (non-working) telephone decorates the wall panelling near the bar.*

MRS M.L.MUDGE LICENSED TO SELL BEERS, WINES & SPIRITS TO BE CONSUMED ON OR OFF THE PREMISES.

# The Drewe Arms

## DREWSTEIGNTON · DEVON

THE MAGNIFICENT wrought iron pub sign standing like a sentinel proclaims the name of its donor, the millionaire Julius Drewe who commissioned Sir Edwin Lutyens to design the famous mock-medieval Castle Drogo, just above the village. Julius Drewe was determined that his village pub would have the best pub sign in the land and the inn, originally The Druid's Arms, was re-named in his honour.

But despite the locals' gratitude – Drewe also had all the village's electric cables buried underground to restore Drewsteignton's appearance to a pre-electric age – this charming inn will be forever be known as Auntie Mabel's after the legendary Mabel Mudge who died not long ago at the venerable age of 101. Mabel was almost certainly England's oldest licensee and was still serving pints aged 99.

Auntie Mabel's face gazes down from photographs in the bars and her name is devotedly picked out on one of the beams inside the pub. Her spirit lingers on in this unadorned interior with its polished country furniture, old photographs and posters and convivial, friendly feeling. Little wonder that

*Opposite: Inside the main bar, with Auntie Mabel's name and licensing details picked out on the beam above the bar. Notice the original stable door, still with its flap. Simple country furniture completes the scene.*

*Left: The magnificent wrought and cast iron sign of The Drewe Arms. Its donor, the millionaire Julius Drewe, was determined that his village pub would have the most magnificent pub sign in the land.*

69

Auntie Mabel's was chosen for an award as "the pub with the most delightful atmosphere".

The building dates back many centuries and was originally two cottages. Features like the old stable doors still survive. Today it has two tiny bars, the public bar and dining room as well as a cool little passageway which perspiring customers use as a drinking area on hot days . . . in winter Auntie Mabel's old Raeburn cooker still provides warmth.

*Opposite: Looking across the main bar to the brick fireplace and walls adorned with old photographs and posters. The poster is for the 1951 sale of farm stock when Auntie Mabel disposed of her stock on her adjoining smallholding to concentrate on running the pub.*

*Left: A surviving bell above a trio of cast iron coat hooks. The bell is a survivor from the days when the pub was also a small hotel.*

*Below left: A forfeit for darts players . . . anyone scoring nine or under must donate a penny to charity.*

*Below: Old photographs and Auntie Mabel's sale poster.*

# The Square & Compass

WORTH MATRAVERS · DORSET

**A** TRADITIONAL OLD FARM CART stands outside The Square and Compass, encouraging passers-by to enjoy the equally period delights inside. The pub, deep in Thomas Hardy country, has been licensed for more than two centuries and run by the Newman family since 1907. The rustic furniture and decor has charmed discerning visitors and locals for many years. London artists including Augustus John had second homes nearby, a connection immortalised in a John sketch of the present owner Charlie Newman's great great grandfather.

Oak panelling, beamed ceilings, country furniture and a fine collection of pictures, old photographs and other mementos blend in reassuring harmony in the busy interiors of the main public bar and smaller Tap Room.

*Above: A traditional farm cart stands outside The Square and Compass in Worth Matravers, Dorset.*
*Opposite: A corner of the Tap Room. Curious visitors enjoy searching the surface of the table for graffiti made by servicemen stationed nearby, including some celebrating VE Day in 1945.*

*Left: A stag's skull found in nearby woodland was hung on these coat hooks as a temporary Halloween party decoration years ago. Somehow it was never taken down.*

*Above right: A view of the main public bar with its oak panelling and beamed ceiling.*

*Right: An old lamp by a photograph of the present owner's great grandfather Charlie Newman when he appeared on TV in the 1940s. Charlie Newman took over the pub in 1907.*

*Below right: Part of the propellor from an old landing craft collected on one of the nearby Ministry of Defence ranges. The picture of a cat is one of ten cat pictures in The Square and Compass's large collection of pictures and photographs.*

*Right: A view of the smaller Tap Room bar with a turned oak seat by one of the plain country tables. The pictures on the wall include a 1939 photograph with locals standing outside the pub and a plaque recording the 70th anniversary of the Newman family's ownership in 1977.*

*Above left: The other end of the Tap Room with a wood stove and fireplace.*

*Below left: The public bar with pictures including a photograph of the original Charlie Newman, a sketch of the artist Augustus John, a celebrated customer, and a sketch by John himself, of his publican Charlie Newman.*

# The King's Head

## VICTORIA STREET · BRISTOL

THREATENED with demolition in the early 1980s but saved by a Grade II listing after a vigorous campaign by regulars, The King's Head emerged like a wondrous butterfly from a dull chrysalis when brewers Courage sent the decorators in. Sixteen layers of emulsion paint were stripped away to reveal a superb Edwardian gold and silver leaf mirror, marble surfaces and a host of other ornaments which had been hidden for generations. This remarkable pub in the shadow of the leaning tower of Temple Church opened in 1660 but its cellars are far older, possibly 12th century. Today's interior is largely early 19th century with a wealth of ornate pub decorations including bar supports overlaid with faded gold leaf details. The very unusual snug at the rear of the pub is shaped like a traditional tramcar, after which it takes its name as the Tramcar Bar. Old gas fittings survive in pristine glory including a pipe lighter, lamp holders and even the original pressure guage which allowed the landlord to brighten the interior at night when the mains pressure fell once the street lights were lit. Small, compact and

*Opposite: The front bar with supporting foliage flourishes below the bar top and a dresser displaying gold leaf signs advertising the drinks on sale. Above: One of the original gas fittings. Many survive here, including an old pipe lighter.*

friendly, The King's Head is a favourite with business people and other regulars who relish the care and attention lavished on preserving every detail of the mahogany brown panelling, decorative woodwork and 19th century signs advertising the range of products on sale from Hollands gin to fine clarets. It is all too rare to praise a brewery for restoring a pub to its original but plaudits are due to Courages - and to an investigative builder who began scratching at old paintwork and saw a gleam of gold.

*Opposite: The tramcar bar at the back of The King's Head, named after its tramcar like lay-out.*

*Above left: The gallery-like display of contemporary photographs and prints of old Bristol fascinate visitors.*

*Below left: One of the gold leaf floral bar supports of varying designs below the main bar top.*

# The Black Horse Hotel

### NORTHFIELD · BIRMINGHAM

WORK ON THE AMBITIOUS SCHEME for a new Black Horse Hotel on Birmingham's busy Bristol Road began in 1912, right next door to a far older Black Horse inn. World War I interrupted the construction of what was planned as the flagship for brewers Davenports and the hotel was not completed until 1929 when the adjoining Black Horse closed its doors for the last time.

Birmingham's period pubs have a character and confidence all of their own, expressed in pride in handsome details, fine workmanship, a strong sense of flamboyance and, frequently, an imaginative mix and match of periods.

Beamed ceilings, elaborate plasterwork, stone carving and other embellishments were all thrown together in an architectural hotpot which cheerfully blends the Edwardian with the Georgian and the Elizabethan with Renaissance Italy. Just as long as a self-confident opulence was achieved to reflect Birmingham's status as the Second City.

The Black Horse, now no longer a hotel, displays all this boisterousness in its bars, restaurant and function rooms, all lovingly presented in much of their original splendour. It is a celebration . . . and a place to celebrate.

*Opposite: The sign of The Black Horse, a delicately carved tondo with a foliate surround decorated with roses. The emblem, about 3 feet in diameter, rears triumphantly above the fireplace in the restaurant.*

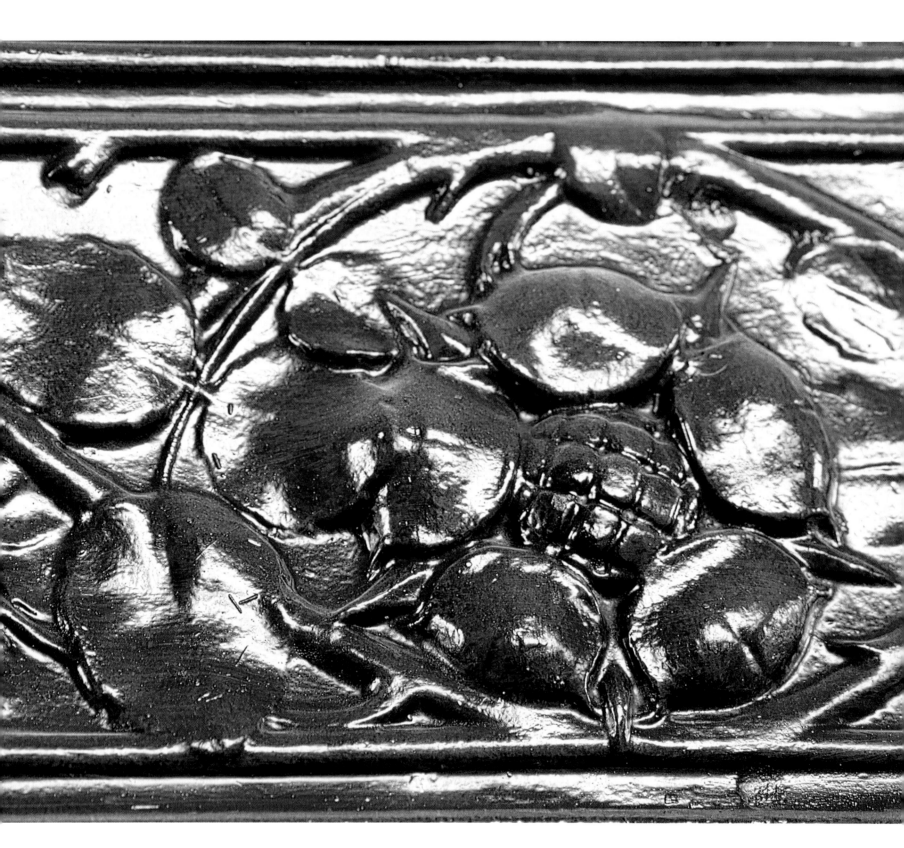

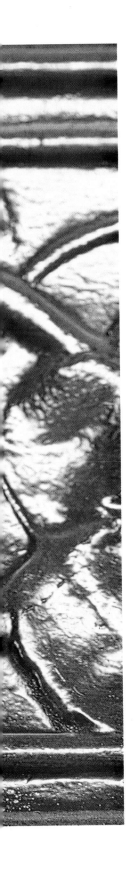

*Opposite: The narrow dado of fruit in relief which is repeated in both wood and plaster throughout The Black Horse Hotel.*

*Above: The lounge area with, above the fireplace, a mirror surrounded by elaborate carving. Below left: The corridor from the restaurant to the garden with touches of mock- Elizabethan. Below right: A detail of the plaster ceiling decoration repeated in several rooms.*

# The Seven Stars

## FALMOUTH · CORNWALL

THE TONGUE-AND-GROOVE clad Seven Stars began trading as a pub in 1660. It has been in the same family since 1873. The present landlord is the colourful Reverend Barrington Bennetts who combines his duties behind the bar with his work as an assistant priest with the Church of England.

The building has remained unchanged since shortly after World War II when his father took down a wall separating the former Smoke Room from the main bar to create more space. Otherwise the simple, sunny interior with its half-panneling and hard-wearing furniture is intact. Pictures, mirrors and, most unusually, a huge collection of key rings being added over the years provide decorative

touches. Years ago a customer left some key rings with brewery connections behind. They were hung in the bar and compulsively added so there are now more than 1000; a most unusual variation on more common pub collections. There is a strong seafaring connection and the family once ran an oyster bar on the premises. A seventy year old paper bag in which oysters were once sold is part of the decoration in the single public bar.

Another reminder is a fine half model of a ship made by one of the regulars complete with a framed legend giving the details of the ship from which the model was made.

Rugged, friendly and down-to-earth, The Seven Stars is a perfect example of a small coastal West Country Victorian pub.

*Above: A corner of the bar.*
*Opposite: A view of the bar looking towards the door. The tongue-and-groove ceiling has the double groove used in the late 19th century . . . when a section had to be replaced not long ago, a local college took on the job as an architectural project.*

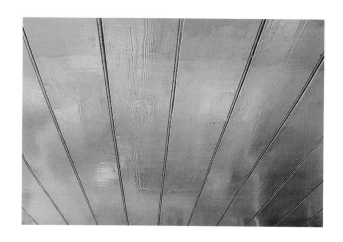

Right: Part of the display at one end of the bar including a handsome advertising mirror, a veteran Guinness clock and the half-model of a ship made by one of The Seven Star's regulars. Below the model is a framed legend describing details of the ship from which it is modelled.

Above left: A close-up of the tongue-and-groove ceiling featuring the double groove that was common in the late 19th century.

Below left: The pub fireplace surrounded by memorabilia including a 70-year-old paper bag dating back to the time the family ran an oyster bar on the premises.

*Left: Part of the pub's collection of more than 1000 key rings started when the present landlord's mother found four key rings during a spring clean, hung them on display in the bar and began a fashion with regulars and visitors who began to contribute rings to add to this very unusual display.*

*Below: A utilitarian shelf in the main bar . . . the fittings have remained unchanged for years and the only post-war alteration in the pub was the removal of a wall between the former Smoke Room and the Public Bar in 1947 to create more space.*

*Bottom: A window looking out on to the Moor outside.*

# The Three Stags Heads

WARDLOW MIRES • NEAR TIDESWELL • DERBYSHIRE

A TRADITIONAL Peak District farming Long House, the Three Stags Heads was built between 1680 and 1700, with living accommodation for the family at one end and covered pens for farm animals at the other. Two rooms were added much later, in the first few years of Queen Victoria's reign.

Today it is a thriving country pub with a host of original features including flagstone floors and a working step grate and side oven which date from about 1840. You'll find 200 and 300-year-old wooden cased locks on some of the doors. The present owners, the Fullers bought the pub in 1988 so that they could successfully combine running and sensitively restoring a fine old country inn with their other interest as working potters, using an adjacent outhouse as pottery. Until they arrived, The Three Stags Heads had been in the same family since 1839.

This very traditional, rough-hewn Peak District pub has two bars, the main bar and the little Victorian dining room which is now named the Music Room. Local folk musicians regularly play here, keeping musical traditions alive just as the Fullers have kept the spirit of the country inn intact.

*Opposite: The simple, sensitively restored interior of the main bar with ladder back chairs and old tables. Many of the original fittings of the building, originally a Long House farm in which the family lived at one end, farm animals at the other, have been preserved including the old kitchen range in the centre of the picture.*

*Left: The handle of an old mincing machine.*

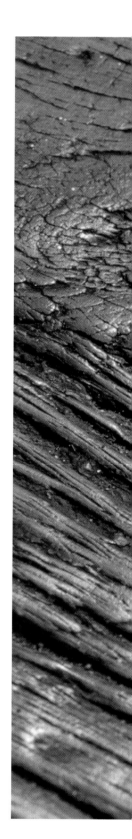

The Three Stags Heads is packed with
details and surfaces grained by years
of use and cleaning.

*Right: The wooden surface of a settle
under the window in the main bar
room, its grains scored by generations
of use. The owners brought it with
them when they took over the pub in
1988.*

*Above left: A brass letter 2 on the
door of the main bar, a relic of the
days when the licensing authorities
insisted that every room in a pub had
to be numbered and listed for the
purpose it was licensed.*

*Below left: A detail of the door by the
fireplace shown on page 93, with the
roughened grain of old lead paint.*

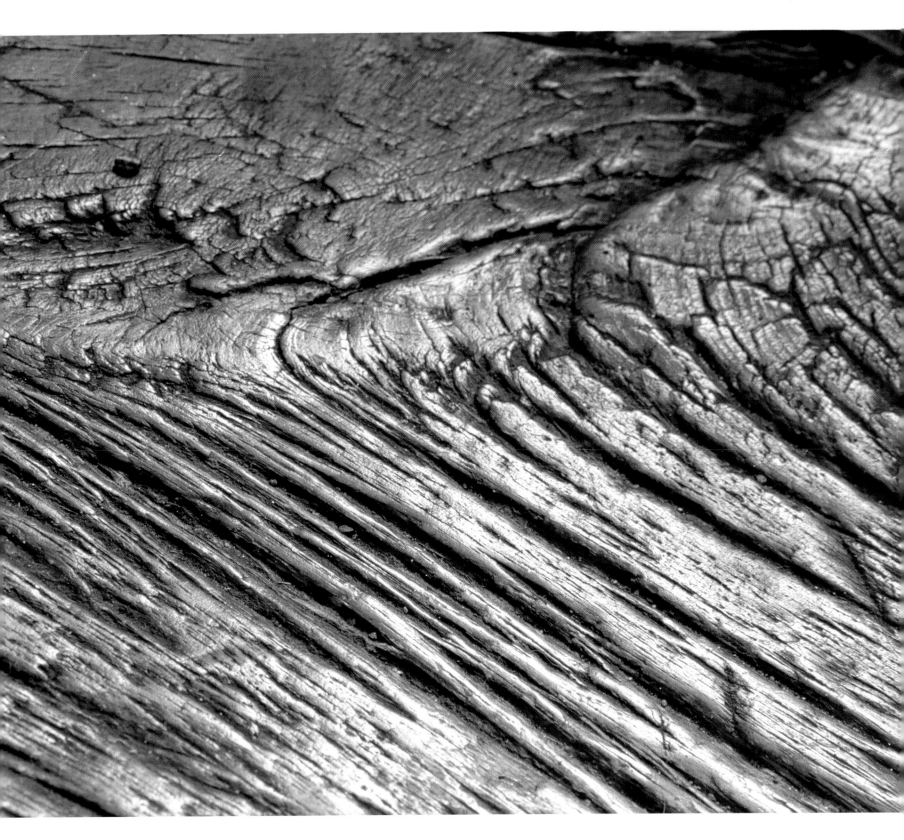

Left: The Music Room, where local folk musicians regularly perform.
Above: A rush-seated ladder-back chair in the main bar, just by the old
fireplace with, to the right, an early stool and a settle resting on the
flagstone floors.
Below: A detail of plates displayed on one of the shelves.
The owners are potters and use the outside barn for their work,
combining pottery with running and restoring the pub.

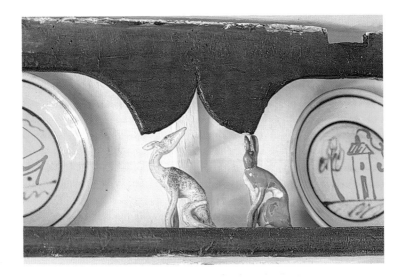

# Barley Mow

## KIRK IRETON · DERBYSHIRE

A SUNDIAL ON THE FRONT WALL of The Barley Mow gives the date 1683 and records show that this handsomely beamed inn in the hilltop village of Kirk Ireton in the Derbyshire Dales close to the Peak District has been a pub for at least 200 years. The single bar serves three separate areas including the Parlour with its Victorian features and furniture.

High backed settles, sturdy country chairs and stools and well-worn tables, including some which have been made from the slate base of a former billiard table, offer visitors a chance to drink in truly traditional surroundings. The beer is served directly from barrels on a stone "thrall" behind the bar with its oak serving counter.

The floors, a mixture of patterned, chequered and terracotta tiles, are particularly noteworthy. Remarkably, when the Shorts took on The Barley Mow in the 1970s, the interiors were completely unfurnished. All they inherited were a coal bucket and a poker.

Years of careful collecting have brought a seamless feel to the decor, with furniture and fittings which harmonise with the spirit of this grand Derbyshire village pub.

*Left: The main bar, one of three at The Barley Mow. The interiors were completely unfurnished when the present owners took over the pub in the 1970s and the traditional look is a tribute to their good taste in collecting suitable old furniture. Above: Barrels resting on the stone thrall.*

*Opposite: A rustic chair casts shadows across a tiled floor. The floors, of terracotta and patterned, chequered tiles are one of the outstanding features of The Barley Mow.*

*Above: One of the stools standing on terracotta tiles by the oak serving counter.*

Opposite: The small beamed room behind the main bar, looking to the doorway, with high-backed settles and unadorned country furniture. The mullioned windows date back to the first half of the 17th century. Above: A corner of one of the pub's slate tables made from the slate surface of a three-quarter sized billiard table. Below: A fire blazes cheerfully in the grate of the open fireplace in the main bar.

# The Ship Hotel

OVERTON · LANCASHIRE

THIS UNSPOILT, multi-roomed Victorian hotel, now only offering B and B but complete with its own crown bowling green stands by the Lune estuary, the haunt of countless wild birds. The connection is preserved when you step into the extraordinary Egg Room with its wonderful collection of wild birds' eggs gathered by locals many years ago when birds-nesting was still legal.

The masterpiece is the central case above the old fireplace with more than 3,500 eggs lovingly set in circles surrounding the central ostrich egg, all clearly labelled by the craftsman who created this remarkable montage. Also on display are stuffed birds and animals in cases, another typically period touch. These souvenirs, so beloved by the Victorian guests who came to stay at The Ship, is echoed throughout with fine old mosaic-topped wrought iron pub tables, a very handsome decorative tiled floor in the lounge and magnficent woodwork on the bar and other fittings, believed to have been supplied by the celebrated furniture makers Waring and Gillows.

The relaxed elegance that made The Ship and its adjoining pleasure gardens a magnet for visitors from Morecambe in its early days remains largely untouched by time and is jealously guarded by today's licensee. And long may it continue to be.

*Opposite: An imposing long case clock stands sentinel in a corner of the extraordinary Egg Room. Above the old fireplace hangs the remarkable case containing more than 3,500 clearly labelled eggs in an arresting display. The rings of smaller eggs surround a single ostrich egg. Above: A detail of a tiled table.*

## Ship Hotel Pleasure Gardens

### OVERTON, near MORECAMBE.

ADMISSION FREE.          Proprietor: JOHN BIRKETT.

The Finest Collection of Birds Eggs in the North. Upwards of 3,5(
British Eggs on view. Also large Cabinet containing upwards
330 varieties—all British.

EVERY ACCOMMODATION FOR CYCLISTS AND VISITOR
BOWLING GREENS AND SWINGS.

LUNCHEONS, DINNERS AND TEAS MADE TO ORDER
LARGE FIELD FOR PICNIC PARTIES.

ne of the most enjoyable Drives from Morecambe is through Heysham t
e old-fashioned village of Overton, returning by the side of the River Lun
ia Snatchems, a grand circular trip of three hours. The Church at Overto
(admitted to be one of the oldest in England) well worth a visit.

*Opposite: The main bar in the lounge of The Ship Hotel. Much of the furniture is original and the very elaborate wooden bar fittings and other decorations are believed to have been supplied by the well-known furniture makers Waring and Gillow.*

*Left: Another view of the Egg Room with a collection of copper jugs suspended from a ceiling beam.*

*Above: An old sign advertising the hotel's pleasure gardens. The hotel boasts its own crown bowling green.*

# The Philharmonic

## HOPE STREET · LIVERPOOL

W HEN the architect Walter Thomas Brevery was commissioned to design a luxurious dining rooms in central Liverpool in 1898, he had a team of outstanding craftsmen and artists on hand to help him achieve his wildest dreams. These were the men from the local shipyards who fitted out the great ocean liners with their sumptuous interiors, each ship vying with the next to be the most ornate in the highly competitive world of ocean travel. The Philharmonic's interiors are land-locked recreations. Expert ceramicists, carpenters, stained glass artists, brass workers, furniture makers and

*Above: Glass and panelling by the side room just inside the main door. The architect Walter Thomas Brevery employed a team of craftsmen and artists trained to fit out the interiors of luxury ocean liners when he created The Philharmonic dining rooms. Right: A detail of the mosaic floor. These decorated floors are found in every room.*

chandelier makers were assembled into a team to provide Liverpool with one of the grandest set of dining rooms in the land. Their creation is truly awe-inspiring. Portraits of contemporary heroes like Field Marshal Lord Roberts and Baden Powell gaze across an interior which is so packed with triumphant flourishes that visitors are at a loss to know what to admire first when they visit The Philharmonic.

Two snugs are named Brahms and Lizst . . . not because of the rhyming slang for "pissed" but in honour of the great 19th century composers whose full-figure portraits are beautifully executed in stained glass windows above.

Rich panelling inset with stained and engraved glass, glorious plaster ceilings and cornices, wonderfully detailed wooden columns and superbly intricate mosaic work which extends up the side of the bar past curving brass foot-rails come together in a riot of late Victorian decoration.

*Above left: A detail of the wood carving on the bar pillars, a typical example of the craftsmanship to be found in every corner of The Philharmonic.*

*Left: The brass handle on the door leading to the Grand Lounge, its interior lit by magnificent chandeliers.*

*Opposite: The main bar with its handsome fireplace topped by an oval mirror and adjoining button-backed leather settles. Above and to the left of the mirror are portraits of Baden Powell and Field Marshal Lord Roberts. The intricate floor mosaics are echoed by the beautifully finished mosaic decoration on the side of the bar itself.*

Opposite: *A detail of the ceramics on the wall leading into the gents. Many women visitors ask for a peep into the gents to admire its grandly decorated walls and fittings.*

Above: *The side of the bar with its mosaic decoration echoing the mosaic floors found throughout The Philharmonic.*

Above right: *A little tulip motif on the mosaic floor.*

Right: *The stained glass full length portrait of the composer Liszt. Another snug is named after Brahms.*

# The Prince Alfred

FORMOSA STREET • MAIDA VALE • LONDON

*Above: A detail of one of the windows overlooking the street.*
*Left: The main bar with the largest snug in the foreground. Note the little inter-connecting door (bottom left) leading from one bar to the next.*

I'D HESITATE to describe The Prince Alfred with all its early Victorian finery in the exotically named Formosa Street as a gin palace but it would be discourteous not to praise this wonderful 1850s pub as anything less than palatial. Elaborately carved and cut wood and glasswork, the sparkle gleam of highly polished brass, an intricate plaster ceiling and an intimate network of little snugs radiating from the central bar delight and enchant visitors as much today as they did in the early years of Queen Victoria's reign.

Standing in a busy corner of prosperous Maida Vale and just a couple of streets away from Little Venice, the pub has a very unusual interior lay-out. Each of the four snugs of varying size has its own door to the street outside and is separated from the next by wood-and-glass panels, some with tilting windows for adjustable privacy. You can only move from one to the next by stepping outdoors or by squeezing through the curious little waist-high inter-connecting doors. A change of bar involves a deep bow to prevent yourself banging your head as you move from one group of drinkers to the next.

The detail throughout the interior is a fantasy of pediments and pillars, miniature balustrades and

brasswork, deeply varnished wooden surfaces and superbly decorated windows decorated with designs of foliage and birds.

Sadly, the upstairs restaurant was destroyed during World War II but the rest remains intact, a timeless reminder of the days when a hard week in wretched surroundings ended with a spree in the escapist, grandiose world of this lavish, lovingly cared-for inn.

*Above: Top, Swivel windows separating one snug from the next. Below, a miniature balustrade above one of the inter-bar screens. Left: The named pub clock above the bar with a gas lamp (right).*

# The Three Horseshoes

## BOROUGHBRIDGE • NORTH YORKSHIRE

THE THREE HORSESHOES is something of a rarity at the close of the 20th century – an unusually well-preserved and maintained early 1930s pub and hotel with utterly authentic period charm. Plush red leather settles, delicate stained glass windows and accommodating furniture in large rooms speak of a more leisurely age than today's.

The Three Horseshoes, which stands on the old A1 trunk road and is in triangle between York, Ripon and Harrogate, is a magnet for discerning drinkers from throughout the area and beyond. The 10-bedroomed hotel was created in 1930 from an earlier pub and a rank of terraced cottages which were demolished to make way for today's hostelry in the thriving North Yorkshire market town of Boroughbridge. The hotel and its pub predecessor have been in the same family since 1900, hence that uninterrupted feel about its decor.

A thriving social centre for locals and visitors alike, the public rooms are adorned with photographs of football teams which once used The Three Horseshoes as

*Opposite: The bay window looking out onto the old A1 trunk road with its stained glass tracery clearly advertising the room's use to encourage passers-by to come inside and enjoy the fare on offer. Comfortable armchairs and an upholstered window seat complete the scene.*

their headquarters. Only minor changes have been made in the last seven decades with later carpets and wallpaper replacing the originals.

There's a strong sense of solidity in the overall design with its oak fireplace and light, traced glasswork. Each room has its own stained glass window inscription describing its purpose to passers-by to encourage them to enjoy the hospitality inside.

*Opposite: A side of the main bar at The Three Horseshoes. The tall, red leather-upholstered settees and other details date back to 1930 when the original pub and adjoining cottages were razed to make way for the then up-to-the-minute roadside hotel. To the right of the dartboard is an old-fashioned darts scoreboard.*

*Above left: The solid oak fireplace in the dining room with a clock advertising Craven A cigarettes.*
*The photograph above the fireplace is of the triumphant Three Horseshoes football team of 1952 which won every major local trophy.*

*Bottom left: The colourful, art nouveau inspired stained glass panels of the door leading to the dining room.*

*Bottom right: an old electric bell button in the lounge which is still in use today. It sounds a bell in the kitchen to alert the staff's attention to hungry or thirsty customers.*

*Opposite: The lounge bar dominated by its old-fashioned fireplace, with the serving bar to the right. The pictures include a photograph of the pub as it was many years ago.*

*Above: A detail showing the three sided alcove seat, clad in red leather, in the bay window of the lounge bar.*

# The Dyffryn Arms

PONTFAEN • WALES

EER IS STILL POURED for customers from a jug in truly traditional style, patriotic pictures dating back to World War I gaze down on the drinkers seated at plain, weathered wooden tables . . . there is a timeless quality about the simple, welcoming charm of The Dyffryn Arms in the tiny valley village of Pontfaen, not far from Fishguard in west Wales.

It comes as little surprise to discover that the pub, which was built as an inn and first licensed in 1845 has been in landlady Bessie Davie's family from the very beginning. Furniture has only been replaced when wear and tear have made it necessary and succeeding generations have jealously guarded the spirit of this place. The Dyffryn Arms offers a small main bar and an even smaller adjoining overspill room to welcome regulars from in and around the village and, in the summer months, visitors to this beautiful, popular corner of Wales. All are charmed by its unpretentious authenticity, from the checkered floor tiles to the comfortable wooden settles and other furniture. The plain, rugged interior reflects the life of the valley and surrounding countryside . . . a rural pub with no frills which has been - and continues to be - a much-loved social centre and a hub of village life for more than a century and a half.

*Above: A detail of the chequered tile floor in the main bar.*

*Opposite: A view of the main bar. The picture, upper left, is titled "The Hardest Goodbye", a patriotic scene of farewell dating back to the First World War.*

*Opposite: Two of the scrubbed, well-worn table tops in the main bar, one oak, the other rosewood. The pub has been in the family since the 1830s and furniture has only been replaced when wear and tear have dictated that new additions were imperative.*

*Above left: A photograph of the Prince of Wales in uniform taken at the time of his investiture. The settle below is a church pew, installed as part of the pub's furniture more than half a century ago.*

*Above right: A corner of the main bar showing the door to the outside passage, the floor tiles and one of the bar's unadorned wooden chairs.*

# The Anchor Inn

HIGH OFFLEY · NEAR WOODSEAVES · STAFFORDSHIRE

*Above: The canal-side Anchor Inn, which has served boat people for more than a century. The canal theme is echoed in many of the pub's decorations with traditional castles and roses.*

*Opposite: A detail showing an original shutter and shutter knob on one of The Anchor's windows.*

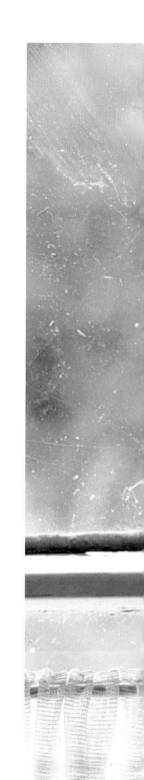

WATER GYPSIES with their fantastically-decorated narrow boats and well-tended horses once shared pints, gossip and music with local villagers in the bars of The Anchor Inn set beside the Shropshire Union canal. Today pleasure craft have replaced the working boats, but the tradition lingers on – though today's boatmen no longer bang on the door to beg for a pint at 6 a.m. as in the old days!

The canal theme is picked up in various parts of the pub, with romantic flourishes of castles and roses which used to adorn first the horse-drawn boats and, later, the mechanised barges and their attached butty boats.

The Anchor has been in the Cliff family for more than a century but its history as a pub is earlier, dating back to the start of the 19th century and perhaps beyond. Canal folk and local farm workers were its mainstay and the recent loss of the stables for the barge-drawing canal horses in a gale is a shame. The Cliffs hope to rebuild it one day.

High-backed settles, well-worn wooden stools and tables and a simple lounge bar with a strong bargee's rose motif echoing the Cliffs' love for the old days when Britain's waterways played such an important part in transport in the pre-motorway age, complete the picture.

*Opposite: The main bar with a frontage lovingly decorated as if it were the cabin-side of a narrow boat. The high backed settle is well over 100 years old.*

*Above: The sculptural wing of the tall settle in the main bar. Below left: The original tiller of a narrow boat, re-painted with a sign for The Anchor. Below right: A detail of the bar frontage. The design is copied from the traditional cabin exterior of a narrow boat, with the rose motif and decorative lettering.*

Opposite: The lounge bar at
The Anchor Inn with its stone-
built open fireplace and simple
furniture. The wallpaper, with its
flourishes of large roses, was
carefully chosen to pick up the
theme of narrow boat decoration.
Castles and roses were the main
motifs used by canal families on
their boats, water jugs and other
equipment.

Above left: The corner of one of
the tables in the main bar, its
surface patinated by many years
of use.

Left: A nest of six well-used stools
in the main bar. The table detail in
the picture above is a corner of the
long table, upper left.

# 'The Case is Altered'

## FIVE WAYS · WARWICKSHIRE

**W**HAT AN ARRESTING NAME . . . enough to encourage the curious, leave alone the real ale fan, to go off the beaten track to unravel the riddle. In fact, the case before the licensing authorities reputedly refers to a second attempt after refurbishment to re-license this delightful Warwickshire country pub so that spirits could be sold. Once the authorities heard of the changes, it was pronounced that the case was altered and permission granted. Time stands still in this centuries-old building, once a cottage, which you'll have to search for diligently near Five Ways on the main Birmingham-Warwick road. The pub's rigid opening hours fly in the face of today's flexible licensing laws and remain firmly fixed under the decrees of World War I, when drinking times were strictly limited to further the war effort. Sunday lunchtime, for example, remains set at 12 noon to 2 p.m., a rare relic of the old days.

An old billiards table from Birmingham provides traditional entertainment, but at an unusual price: punters must use old 6d – sixpenny – pieces to operate it. The till firmly refuses to adopt decimalisation and still records sales in pounds, shillings and pence. But don't worry, today's money will be gratefully accepted if curiously rung up.

The interior is a rich mixture of dark, ages old wood, beams, nicotene-stained walls and an old fashioned cluster of furniture to give warmth and welcome to all who visit.

*Opposite. A detail of the 100-year-old billiard table in the small billiards room. It is still operated with pre-decimalisation sixpenny pieces.*

*Above: the bar with, centre right, a poster for brewers Lucas Blackwell and Arkwright of Leamington Spa.*

Opposite: The main bar with its beamed ceiling. This was once the main room of a country cottage. Above: The window in the lounge bar. Below left: The old till which still records the takings in old-fashioned pounds, shillings and pence. Like the opening times, the records remain firmly fixed in the past. Below right: The corner of one of the picture frames. Old brewery posters adorn the walls.

These pubs are of outstanding historic interest and as such are on CAMRA's National Inventory of intact or little altered heritage pubs. The full list is given here as well as the full address of each outstanding pub

## ENGLAND

### BEDFORDSHIRE
Broom: *Cock*, 23 High Street

### BERKSHIRE
Aldworth: *Bell*, Bell Lane (off B4009)
Frilsham: *Pot Kiln*
(Yattendon–Bucklebury road)

### CHESHIRE
Alpraham: *Travellers Rest*, Chester Road (A51)
Barthomley: *White Lion*, Audley Road
Gawsworth: *Harrington Arms*,
Congleton Road
Macclesfield: *Castle*, Churchwallgate
Stockton Heath: *Red Lion*, London Road
Wheelock: *Commercial*, Game Street

### CORNWALL
Falmouth: *Seven Stars*, The Moor

### CUMBRIA
Broughton Mills: *Blacksmiths Arms*
Kendal: *Ring O'Bells*, 39 Kirkland

### DERBYSHIRE
Brassington: *Gate Inn*, Well Street
Derby: *Old Dolphin*, Queen Street
Elton: *Duke of York*, West End
Kirk Ireton: *Barley Mow*, Main Street
Wardlow Mires: *Three Stags Heads*
(at A623/B6465 junction)

### DEVON
Drewsteignton: *Drewe Arms*, The Square
Holsworthy: *Kings Arms*, Fore Street
Luppitt: *Luppitt Inn*
Topsham: *Bridge*, Bridge Hill
Widecombe-in-the-Moor: *Rugglestone Inn*
(1/4 mile south of village)

### DORSET
Worth Matravers: *Square & Compass*
(off B3069)

### DURHAM
Durham City: *Shakespeare*, 63 Saddler Street
*Victoria*, 86 Hallgarth Street

### GLOUCESTERSHIRE & BRISTOL
Ampney St Peter: *Red Lion* (on A417)
Bristol: *Kings Head*, 60 Victoria Street
Cheltenham: *Bath Tavern*, 68 Bath Road
Duntisbourne Abbots: *Five Mile House*,
Gloucester Road (A417)
Purton: *Berkeley Arms*
Willsbridge: *Queens Head*, 62 Bath Road

### HAMPSHIRE
Steep: *Harrow*, Harrow Lane

### HEREFORDSHIRE
Kington: *Olde Tavern*, 22 Victoria Road
Leintwardine: *Sun Inn*, Rosemary Lane
Risbury: *Hop Pole* (Bert's),
on Pencombe Road

### KENT
Cowden Pound: *Queens Arms*,
Hartfield Road (on B2026)
Ightam: *Old House*, Redwell Lane
Snargate: *Red Lion*, (on B2080)

### LANCASHIRE
Brierfield: *Waggon & Horses*, Colne Road
Great Harwood: *Victoria*, St John Street
Overton: *Ship Hotel*, 9 Main Street
Preston: *Black Horse*, 166 Friargate
Waddington: *(Lower) Buck*, Church Road

### LEICESTERSHIRE & RUTLAND
Medbourne: *Horse & Trumpet*, Old Green

### GREATER LONDON
EC1 Hatton Garden: *Old Mitre*, Ely Court,
9 Ely Place
EC4 Blackfriars: *Black Friar*,
174 Queen Victoria Street
WC1 Holborn: *Cittie of York*,
22 High Holborn
*Princess Louise*, 208 High Holborn

WC2 Covent Garden: *Lamb & Flag*,
33 Rose Street
*Salisbury*, 90 St Martins Lane

E14 Poplar: *Grapes*, 76 Narrow St

N4 Finsbury Park: *Salisbury*,
1 Grand Parade, Green Lanes
N6 Highgate: *Flask*, 77 Highgate West Hill
N8 Hornsey: *Gt Northern Railway*,
67 High Street

NW3 Hampstead: *Holly Bush*,
22 Holly Mount
NW6 Kilburn: *Black Lion*,
274 Kilburn High Road
NW8 St Johns Wood: *Crockers*,
24 Aberdeen Place

SE1 Southwark: *George Inn*,
77 Borough High Street
SE21 Dulwich: *Crown & Greyhound*,
73 Dulwich Village

SW1 Belgravia: *Antelope*, 22 Eaton Terrace
*Nags Head*, 53 Kinnerton Street
*Paxtons Head*, 153 Knightsbridge
SW1 St James's: *Red Lion*,
2 Duke of York Street

W1 Marylebone: *Barley Mow*, 8 Dorset Street
W1 Soho: *Argyll Arms*, 18 Argyll Street
W6 Hammersmith: *Dove*, 19 Upper Mall
W9 Maida Vale: *Prince Alfred*,
5a Formosa Street
*Warrington Hotel*, 93 Warrington Crescent

### GREATER MANCHESTER
Altrincham: *Railway*, 153 Manchester Road,
Broadheath
Bolton: *Howcroft*, Clarence Court
Eccles: *Grapes*, 439 Liverpool Road
*Lamb*, 33 Regent Street
*Royal Oak*, Barton Lane
Gorton: *Plough*, Hyde Road
Heaton Norris: *Nursery Inn*, Green Lane
(off A6)
Manchester: *Britons Protection*, 50 Great
Bridgewater Street
*Circus Tavern*, 86 Portland Street

*Crown & Kettle*, Oldham Road
*Hare & Hounds*, 46 Shudehill
*Mr Thomas's*, 52 Cross Street
*Peveril of the Peak*, 127 Great Bridgewater
Street
Marple: *Hatter Arms*, Church Lane
Middleton: *Old Boars Head*, Long Street
Mossley: *Colliers Arms*, Broadcarr Lane
Rochdale: *Cemetery Hotel*, 470 Bury Road
Stalybridge: *Station Buffet*, Railway Station
Stockport: *Alexandra*, 195 Northgate Road
*Arden Arms*, 23 Millgate
*Queens Head*, 12 Little Underbank
*Swan with Two Necks*, 36 Princes Street
Wigan: *Springfield Hotel*, 47 Springfield Road

### MERSEYSIDE
Birkenhead: *Stork Hotel*, 41-43 Price Street
Liverpool: *Lion*, 67 Moorfield
*Philharmonic*, 36 Hope Street
*Prince Arthur*, 93 Rice Lane, L9
*Vines*, 81 Lime Street
Lydiate: *Scotch Piper*, 347 Southport Road

### NOTTINGHAMSHIRE
Nottingham: *Olde Trip to Jerusalem*,
1 Brewhouse Yard, Castle Road
*Stag & Pheasant*, 245 Parliament St
*Vale Hotel*, Thackeray's Lane, Woodthorpe
West Bridgford: *Test Match Hotel*,
Gordon Square, Gordon Road

### NORTHUMBERLAND
Berwick upon Tweed: *Free Trade*, Castlegate
Netherton: *Star Inn*

### OXFORDSHIRE
Banbury: *Wine Vaults*, 5 & 6 Parson Street
Checkendon: *Black Horse*, Burncote Lane
(off A4074)
Christmas Common: *Fox & Hounds*
(off B480/B481 and B4009)
Steventon: *North Star*, 2 Stocks Lane
Stoke Lyne: *Peyton Arms* (off B3069)
Stoke Row: *Crooked Billet*, Nottwood Lane
Stoke Talmage: *Red Lion*
Wantage: *Shoulder of Mutton*,
38 Wallingford Street

**SHROPSHIRE**

Halfway House: *Seven Stars* (on A458)
Selattyn: *Cross Keys*, (on B4579)
Shrewsbury: *Loggerheads*, 1 Church Street

**SOMERSET**

Appley: *Globe*
Bath: *Old Green Tree*, 12 Green St
*Star*, 23 The Vineyards
Crowcombe: *Carew Arms* (off A358)
Faulkland: *Tuckers Grave Inn*, Wells Road
(A366)
Huish Episcopi: *Rose & Crown* (Eli's),
by Pounsell Lane
Midsomer Norton: *White Hart*, The Island
Norton St Philip: *George*, The Plain
Witham Friary: *Seymour Arms* (off B3092)

**STAFFORDSHIRE**

High Offley: *Anchor*, Old Lea (by canal)

**SUFFOLK**

Brent Eleigh: *Cock*, Lavenham Road
Bury St Edmunds: *Nutshell*, 17 The Traverse
Ipswich: *Golden Hind*, Nacton Road
*Margaret Catchpole*, Cliff Lane
Laxfield: *Kings Head* (Low House), Goram's
Mill Lane
Pin Mill: *Butt & Oyster*, The Quay

**SUSSEX (East)**

Berwick: *Cricketers Arms*
(off A27)

**SUSSEX (West)**

The Haven: *Blue Ship* (at Rudgwick, off A281)

**TYNE & WEAR**

Newcastle-upon-Tyne: *Crown Posada*,
31 The Side

**WARWICKSHIRE**

Five Ways: *Case is Altered*, Case Lane,
off Fiveways Lane
Long Itchington: *Buck & Bell*, Green End

**WEST MIDLANDS**

Birmingham: *Anchor*, 308 Bradford St,
Digbeth
*Bartons Arms*, 152 High Street, Aston

*Bellefield*, 36 Winson Street, Winson Green
*Black Horse*, Bristol Road, Northfield
*Britannia*, 287 Lichfield Road
*British Oak*, Pershore Road, Stirchley
*Market Tavern*, 210-212 Moseley Street,
Digbeth
*Red Lion*, Soho Road, Handsworth
*Rose Villa Tavern*, Warstone Lane
*Samson & Lion*, Yardley Green Road,
Small Heath
*Three Magpies*, Shirley Road, Hall Green
*White Swan*, 276 Bradford Street, Digbeth
*Woodman*, 106 Albert Street, Digbeth
*Villa Tavern*, 307 Nechells Park Road, Nechells
Bloxwich: *Turf Tavern*,
13 Wolverhampton Road
Dudley: *Shakespeare*, Stepping Stone Street
Rushall: *Manor Arms*, Park Road, Daw End
Sedgley: *Beacon*, 129 Bilston Street
Smethwick: *Waterloo Hotel*, Shireland Road

**WILTSHIRE**

Easton Royal: *Bruce Arms* (on B3087)
Salisbury: *Haunch of Venison*, 1 Minster Street

**WORCESTERSHIRE**

Bretforton: *Fleece*, The Cross
Defford: *Cider House* (Monkey House)
(on A4104, Woodmancote)

**YORKSHIRE (East)**

Beverley: *White Horse* (Nellie's),
22 Hengate
Hull: *Olde White Harte*, 25 Silver Street
Skerne: *Eagle Inn*, Wandsford Road

**YORKSHIRE (North)**

Beck Hole: *Birch Hall Inn* (1 mile north of
Goathland)
Boroughbridge: *Three Horse Shoes*,
Bridge Street
Harrogate: *Gardeners Arms*, Bilton Lane
Saxton: *Greyhound*, Main Street
York: *Blue Bell*, 53 Fossgate

**YORKSHIRE (West)**

Bradford: *Cock & Bottle*, 93 Barkerend Road
*New Beehive*, 171 Westgate
Heath: *Kings Arms*, Heath Common
Leeds: *Adelphi*, 1 Hunslet Road

*Cardigan Arms*, 364 Kirkstall Road, Burley
*Garden Gate*, 37 Waterloo Road, Hunslet
*Rising Sun*, 290 Kirkstall Road, Burley
*Whitelocks*, Turks Head Yard, Briggate
Wakefield: *Redoubt*, 28 Horbury Road

---

## WALES

**GWENT**

Abergavenny: *Hen & Chickens*, 7-9 Flannel
Street
Grosmont: *Cupid's Hill Inn* (on B434)

**MID WALES**

Hay on Wye: *Three Tuns*, 4 Broad Street
Llanfihangel-yng-Ngwynfa: *Goat*
Welshpool: *Grapes*, Salop Road

**WEST WALES**

Llandovery: *Red Lion*, 2 Market Square
Pontfaen: *Dyffryn Arms* (off B4313)

---

## SCOTLAND

**THE BORDERS**

Ancrum: *Cross Keys*, The Green

**FIFE**

Kirkaldy: *Feuars Arms*, 66 Commercial Street

**GRAMPIAN**

Aberdeen: *Grill*, 213 Union Street

**THE LOTHIANS**

Dirleton: *Castle*, Manse Road
Edinburgh: *Abbotsford*, 3-5 Rose Street
*Bennets Bar*, 8 Leven Street
*Cafe Royal*, West Register Street
*Kenilworth*, 152-154 Rose Street
*Leslie's Bar*, 45 Ratcliffe Terrace
*Oxford Bar*, 8 Young Street

**STRATHCLYDE**

Glasgow: *Horseshoe Bar*, 17-21 Drury Street
*Old Toll Bar*, 1-3 Paisley Road West
Lochgilphead: *Commercial* (The Comm),
Lochnell Street
Paisley: *Bull*, 7 New Street

Shettleston: *Portland Arms*,
1169 Shettleston Road
Uddingstone: *Rowan Tree*, 60 Old Mill Road

**TAYSIDE**

Dundee: *Clep*, 92-98 Clepington Road
*Speedwell*, 165-7 Perth Road

---

## NORTHERN IRELAND

**COUNTY ANTRIM**

Ballycastle: *House of McDonnell*,
71 Castle Street
Ballyclare: *Carmichael's*, 16 Ballyeaston Village
Bushmills: *Charles H Callaghan*,
72-74 Main Street
Cushendun: *Mary McBride's*, Main Street

**COUNTY ARMAGH**

Portadown: *McConville's*, West Street

**BELFAST**

*Dan Magennis's* (Bradan Bar), May Street
*Crown Liquor Saloon*, 49 Great Victoria Street

**COUNTY FERMANAGH**

Enniskillen: *Blake's Bar*, 6 Church Street

*This list is being continually updated and
a current list is available from CAMRA,
230 Hatfield Road, St Albans,
Herts AL1 4LW*

# CAMRA Books

The CAMRA Books range of guides helps you search out the best in beer (and cider) and brew it at home too!

## Buying in the UK

All our books are available through bookshops in the UK. If you can't find a book, simply order it from your bookshop using the ISBN number, title and author details given below. CAMRA members should refer to their regular monthly newspaper What's Brewing for the latest details and member special offers. CAMRA books are also available by mail-order (postage free) from: CAMRA Books, 230 Hatfield Road, St Albans, Herts, AL1 4LW. Cheques made payable to CAMRA Ltd. Telephone your credit card order on 01727 867201.

## Buying outside the UK

CAMRA books are also sold in many book and beer outlets in the USA and other English-speaking countries. If you have trouble locating a particular book, use the details below to order by mail or fax (+44 1727 867670).

Carriage of £3.00 per book (Europe) and £6.00 per book (US, Australia, New Zealand and other overseas) is charged.

## UK Booksellers

Call CAMRA Books for distribution details and book list. CAMRA Books are listed on all major CD-ROM book lists and on our Internet site: http://www.camra.org.uk

## Overseas Booksellers

Call or fax CAMRA Books for details of local distributors.

Distributors are required for some English language territories. Rights enquiries (for non-English language editions) should be addressed to the managing editor.

# CAMRA Guides

Painstakingly researched and checked, these guides are the leaders in their field, bringing you to the door of pubs which serve real ale and more...

## Good Pub Food

### by Susan Nowak

448 pages          Price: £9.99

The pubs in these pages serve food as original and exciting as anything available in far more expensive restaurants. And, as well as the exotic and unusual, you will find landlords and landladies serving simple, nourishing pub fare such as a genuine ploughman's lunch or a steak and kidney pudding.

You'll discover cooking from a new wave of young chefs who would prefer to run a pub than a restaurant. Many pubs are producing the traditional dishes of their regions, building smokeries, keeping cattle and goats, growing vegetables and herbs, creating vibrant, modern cuisine from fresh ingredients. Recipes from some of them are dotted about this guide so you can try them at home.

Award-winning food and beer writer Susan Nowak, who has travelled

the country to complete this fifth edition of the guide, says that 'eating out' started in British inns and taverns and this guide is a contribution to an appreciation of all that is best in British food...and real cask conditioned ale.

*Use the following code to order this book from your bookshop: ISBN 1-85249-151-5*

## Room at the Inn

### by Jill Adam

242 pages          Price: £8.99

From the first pub claiming to have sold Stilton cheese to travellers in 1720 to old smugglers haunts in Dorset, Room at the Inn gives details of pubs up and down the country offering generous hospitality. Travellers and tourists looking for a traditional British alternative to bland impersonal hotels need look no further than this guide.

The guide contains almost 350 inns – plus some hotels and motels – which provide overnight accommodation and a wholesome English breakfast. Some have been welcoming visitors for centuries. You'll also find a good pint of real ale on your arrival. To help you further there are maps, information on pub meals, family facilities, local tourist attractions and much more. Room at the Inn is a must for the glove compartment of the family car and vital reading for anyone planning a bed and breakfast break, sports tour or business trip.

*Use the following code to order this book from your bookshop: ISBN 1-85249-150-7*

## Real Cider Guide

### by Ted Bruning

256 pages          Price: £7.99

Cider is making a major comeback and Real Cider is worth seeking out wherever you are. This guide helps you find one of Britain's oldest, tastiest and most fascinating drinks. Cider has been made in Britain since before Roman times. But most cider you find in pubs today has been pasteurised, with carbon dioxide added. The resulting drink bears little resemblance to the full-flavoured taste of traditional Real Cider.

Reading this guide makes your mouth water as you leaf through details of more than 2000 pubs selling the real stuff. There are also many farmhouse producers from all over the country and outlets for Cider's equally drinkable cousin, Perry – if you bring a container. Some will even sell you a container! Author Ted Bruning is the editor of the Cider Press, a quarterly supplement to What's Brewing, CAMRA's national newspaper. He has collated information from all over the UK to give you a taste of this fine traditional drink. So why not join him and savour a wealth of different flavours?

*Use the following code to order this book from your bookshop: ISBN 1-85249-121-3*

## Pubs for Families

### by David Perrot

256 pages          Price: £8.99

Traditional pubs with CAMRA-approved ale and a warm welcome for the kids! Nothing could be better. But where to find such a hospitable hostel on home patch, let alone when out and about or on holiday?

This guide is the adult answer to your eating and drinking requirements, with facilities for your children too! Invaluable national coverage with easy to use symbols so that you know what facilities are available and regional maps so you'll know how to get there. Get the best of both worlds.

*Use the following code to order this book from your bookshop: ISBN 1-85249-141-8*

## 50 Great Pub Crawls

*by Barrie Pepper*

*256 pages          Price: £9.99*

Visit the beer trails of the UK, from town centre walks, to hikes and bikes and a crawl on a train on which the pubs are even sited on your side of the track!

Barrie Pepper, with contributions and recommendations from CAMRA branches, has compiled a 'must do' list of pub crawls, with easy to use colour maps to guide you, notes on architecture, history and brewing tradition to entertain you. All you have to do is to move your legs and arms! A great way to discover the pubs of Britain. Use it well and we'll make it the first of a series.

*Use the following code to order this book from your bookshop: ISBN 1-85249-142-6*

## Good Beer Guides

These are comprehensive guides researched by professional beer writers and CAMRA enthusiasts. Use these guides to find the best beer on your travels or to plan your itinerary for the finest drinking. Travel and accommodation information, plus maps, help you on your way and there's plenty to read about the history of brewing, the beer styles and the local cuisine to back up the entries for bars and beverages.

### Good Beer Guide to Munich and Bavaria

*by Graham Lees*

*206 pages          Price: £8.99*

A fifth of the world's breweries – some 750 – are located in the region covered by this guide. The beers have rich, deep flavours and aromas and are generously hopped. You will find dark lagers, wheat beers, members of the ale family, wonderfully quenching and refreshing beers that have become cult drinks. The guide tells you where to find the best beers and the many splendid bars, beer halls and gardens, and the food to match. You'll also find all the background information for the world's most famous beer extravaganza, the Munich Oktoberfest.

Author Graham Lees, a founder member of CAMRA, has lived and worked in Munich for several years and has endlessly toured Bavaria in search of the perfect pint.

*Use the following code to order this book from your bookshop: ISBN 1-85249-114-0*

### Good Beer Guide to Belgium, Holland and Luxembourg

*by Tim Webb*

*286 pages          Price: £9.99*

Discover the stunning range and variety of beers available in the Low Countries, our even nearer neighbours via Le Tunnel. There are such revered styles as Trappist Ales, fruit beers, wheat beers and the lambic and gueuze specialities made by the centuries-old method of spontaneous fermentation.

Channel-hopping Tim Webb's latest edition of the guide offers even more bars in which an incredible array of beers can be enjoyed. If you are going on holiday to this region then you'll find details of travel, accommodation, food, beer museums, brewery visits and festivals, as well as guides to the cafés, beer shops and warehouses you can visit. There are maps, tasting notes, beer style guide and a beers index to complete the most comprehensive companion to drinking with your Belgian and Dutch hosts.

*Use the following code to order this book from your bookshop: ISBN 1-85249-139-6*

### Good Beer Guide to Northern France

*by Arthur Taylor*

*256 pages          Price: £7.99*

Discover the excitement of the bars and cafes, the tranquility of the village breweries which hold the secrets of generations of traditional brewing. Join the many festivals and cultural events such as the beer-refreshed second-hand market in Lille and the presentation of the Christmas ales. Find out where the best beer meets the best mussels and chips. Cuisine a la bière and more! Arthur Taylor is a leading authority on French beer and a member of Les Amis de la Bière, who have co-operated in the research for this book.

*Use the following code to order this book from your bookshop: ISBN 1-85249-140-X*

### Good Beer Guide

*edited by Jon Preece*

*546 pages          Price: £10.99*

Fancy a pint? Let CAMRA's Good Beer Guide lead the way. Revised each year to include around 5,000 great pubs serving excellent ale – country pubs, town pubs and pubs by the sea.

The guide includes information about meals, accommodation, family rooms, no-smoking areas and much more.

Fully and freshly researched by members of the Campaign for Real Ale, real enthusiasts who use the pubs week in, week out. No payment is ever taken for inclusion. The guide has location maps for each county and you can read full details of all Britain's breweries (big and small) and the ales they produce, including tasting notes.

CAMRA's Good Beer Guide is still Britain's best value pub guide – a must for anyone who loves beer and pubs.

## Known Gems & Hidden Treasures – A Pocket Guide to the Pubs of London

*by Peter Haydon*

*224 pages          Price: £7.99*

If you live in or visit London, then you need this guide in your top pocket! It will take you to the well-known and historic pubs you must not miss, but also to the pubs which are tucked away and which locals keep to themselves.

The grass roots organisation of CAMRA and beer journalist Peter Haydon have brought London's pubs alive through their descriptions of ale, food, entertainment, history and architecture. These pubs have a story to tell.

The pubs in this pocket, portable, guide are listed by locality with a street address and London postal code districts heading pages so that you can easily match your location with the nearest pub. The guide covers pubs which are near tube and railway stations and gives relevant bus route numbers. It covers central London out to the commuter belts of Bushey and Surbiton.

*Use the following code to order this book from your bookshop:*
*ISBN 1-85249-118-3*

## Cellarmanship

*by Ivor Clissold*

*144 pages          Price: £6.99*

This book explains every aspect of running a good cellar and serving a great pint of real ale which does both  pub and brewer proud. It's a must have book for all professionals in the drinks trade, for all those studying at college  to join it, and for all those who need to tap a cask of real ale for a party.

The CAMRA Guide to Cellarmanship is the only manual dealing with the care of all cask beers. It draws together information previously only known within certain breweries, and adds valuable experience from hundreds of cellar and technical staff.

Farmers, hop growers, maltsters, brewers and drayers all play their part to produce and deliver our great British drink but too often it falls at the last fence: indifferent cellar and bar management – especially in the face of an unknown guest beer – can turn a  treat into a tragedy.

*Use the following code to order this book from your bookshop:*
*ISBN 1-85249-126-4*

## Good Beer Guide to Prague & Czech Republic

*by Graham Lees*

*256 pages          Price: £8.99*

A comprehensive tour of one of the traditonal brewing centres of Europe. Tour around the many breweries and beer outlets in the company of Graham Lee's tasting notes, maps, tourist information and language guide and make your stay complete. Find out about the brewing history, local ingredients and the politics and economics of brewing which threatens what the Czech people have built over the centuries. Covers pubs, beers, accomodation and food.

*Use the following code to order this book from your bookshop:*
*ISBN 1-85249-122-1*

## Brew Your Own

Learn the basics of brewing real ales at home from the experts. And then move on to more ambitious recipes which imitate well-loved ales from the UK and Europe.

## Brew your own Real Ale at Home

*by Graham Wheeler and Roger Protz*

*194 pages          Price: £8.99*

This book is a treasure chest for all real ale fans and home brew enthusiasts. It contains recipes which allow you to replicate some famous cask-conditioned beers at home or to customise brews to your own particular taste. The authors have examined the ingredients and brewing styles of well-known ales and have gleaned important information from brewers, with and without their co-operation. Computer-aided guesswork and an expert palate have filled in the gaps where the brewers would reveal no more.

As well as the recipes, the brewing process is explained along with the equipment required, all of which allows you to brew beer using wholly natural ingredients. Detailed recipes and instructions are given along with tasting notes for each ale. Conversion details are given so that the measurements can be used world-wide.

*Use the following code to order this book from your bookshop:*
*ISBN 1-85249-138-8*

## Brew Classic European Beers at Home

*by Graham Wheeler and Roger Protz*

*196 pages          Price: £8.99*

Keen home brewers can now recreate some of the world's classic beers. In your own home you can brew superb pale ales, milds, porters, stouts, Pilsners, Alt, Kolsch, Trappist, wheat beers, sour beers, even the astonishing fruit lambics of Belgium… and many more.

Graham Wheeler and his computer have teamed up with Roger Protz and his unrivalled knowledge of brewing and beer styles. Use the detailed recipes and information about ingredients to imitate the cream of international beers. Discover the role played by ingredients, yeasts and brewing equipment and procedure in these well-known drinks. Measurements are given in UK, US and European units, emphasising the truly international scope of the beer styles within.

*Use the following code to order this book from your bookshop:*
*ISBN 1-85249-117-5*

## Home Brewing

*by Graham Wheeler*

*240pages      Price: £8.99*

Recently redesigned to make it even easier to use, this is the classic first book for all home-brewers. While being truly comprehensive, Home Brewing also manages to be a practical guide which can be followed step by step as you try your first brews. Plenty of recipes for beginners and hints and tips from the world's most revered home brewer.

*Use the following code to order this book from your bookshop:*
*ISBN 1-85249-137-X*

# *Joining* CAMRA

If you like good beer and good pubs you could be helping to fight to preserve, protect and promote them. CAMRA was set up in the early seventies to fight against the mass destruction of a part of Britain's heritage.

The giant brewers are still pushing through takeovers, mergers and closures of their smaller regional rivals. They are still trying to impose national brands of beer and lager on their customers whether they like it or not, and they are still closing down town and village pubs or converting them into grotesque 'theme' pubs.

CAMRA wants to see genuine free competition in the brewing industry, fair prices, and, above all, a top quality product brewed by local breweries in accordance with local tastes, and served in pubs that maintain the best features of a tradition that goes back centuries.

As a CAMRA member you will be able to enjoy generous discounts on CAMRA products and receive the highly rated monthly newspaper What's Brewing. You will be given the CAMRA members' handbook and be able to join in local social events and brewery trips.

To join, complete the form below and, if you wish, arrange for direct debit payments by filling in the form overleaf and returning it to CAMRA. To pay by credit card, contact the membership secretary on (01727) 867201.

I/We wish to join the Campaign for Real Ale and agree to abide by the Rules.

Name(s)_____

Address_____

_____

_____Postcode_____

Signature_____Date_____

I/We enclose the remittance for:

Single: £14 ☐     Joint: £17 (at same address) ☐

OAP Single: £8 ☐     OAP Joint: £11 (at same address) ☐

Unemployed/Disabled: £8 ☐

Under 26: £8 ☐     date of birth

For Life and Overseas rates please contact CAMRA HQ
(tel: 01727 867201)

Send you remittance (payable to CAMRA) to:
**The Membership Secretary, CAMRA, 230 Hatfield Road, St Albans, Herts., AL1 4LW**

**SEE REVERSE SIDE FOR DIRECT DEBIT FORM**

Please fill in the whole form using a ball point pen and send it to:

**Campaign for Real Ale Ltd,**
**230 Hatfield Road,**
**St. Albans,**
**Herts**
**AL1 4LW**

## Instruction to your Bank or Building Society to pay by Direct Debit

Originator's Identification Number

| 9 | 2 | 6 | 1 | 2 | 9 |
|---|---|---|---|---|---|

Reference Number

| | | | | | | | | | | | | | | | | | |
|---|---|---|---|---|---|---|---|---|---|---|---|---|---|---|---|---|---|

Name of Account Holder(s)

Bank/Building Society account number

| | | | | | | | |
|---|---|---|---|---|---|---|---|

Branch Sort Code

| | | | | | |
|---|---|---|---|---|---|

Name and full postal address of your Bank or Building Society

| To The Manager | Bank/Building Society |
|---|---|
| Address | |
| | |
| | Postcode |

FOR CAMRA OFFICIAL USE ONLY
This is not part of the instruction to your Bank or Building Society

Membership Number

Name

Postcode

**Instructions to your Bank or Building Society**
Please pay CAMRA Direct Debits from the account detailed on this instruction subject to the safeguards assured by the Direct Debit Guarantee. I understand that this instruction may remain with CAMRA and, if so, will be passed electronically to my Bank/Building Society

| Signature(s) |
|---|
| Date |

Banks and Building Societies may not accept Direct Debit instructions for some types of account

---

**This guarantee should be detached and retained by the Payer.**

## The Direct Debit Guarantee

- This Guarantee is offered by all Banks and Building Societies that take part in the Direct Debit Scheme. The efficiency and security of the Scheme is monited and protected by your own Bank or Building Society.

- If the amounts to be paid or the payment dates change CAMRA will notify you 10 working days in advance of your account being debited or as otherwise agreed.

- If an error is made by CAMRA or your Bank or Building Society, you are guaranteed a full and immediate refund from your branch of the amount paid.

- You can cancel a Direct Debit at any time by writing to your Bank or Building Society. Please also send a copy of your letter to us.